2009 SUPPLEMENT

to

SCIENTIFIC EVIDENCE IN CIVIL AND CRIMINAL CASES

By

ANDRE A. MOENSSENS, J.D., LL.M.
Douglas Stripp Professor of Law Emeritus
University of Missouri at Kansas City
Professor of Law Emeritus, University of Richmond
Forensic Consultant

CAROL E. HENDERSON, J.D.
Director, National Clearinghouse for Science, Technology and Law
Stetson University College of Law

and

SHARON G. PORTWOOD, J.D., Ph.D.
Executive Director, Institute for Social Capital
Professor of Health Behavior & Administration
University of North Carolina, Charlotte

FIFTH EDITION

FOUNDATION PRESS
2009

THOMSON REUTERS

© 2009 By THOMSON REUTERS/FOUNDATION PRESS

  195 Broadway, 9th Floor

  New York, NY 10007

  Phone Toll Free 1–877–888–1330

  Fax (212) 367–6799

  foundation–press.com

Printed in the United States of America

ISBN 978–1–59941–333–4

TABLE OF CONTENTS

TABLE OF CONTENTS

CHAPTER 2.   DEMONSTRATIVE EVIDENCE

I.   Introduction

CHAPTER 3.   CHEMICAL AND OTHER TESTS FOR ALCOHOLIC INTOXICATION

I.   Alcohol Intoxication Testing

TABLE OF CONTENTS

III. Miscellaneous

CHAPTER 4. SCIENTIFIC DETECTION OF SPEEDING

II. Radar Speed Detection

V. Evidence of Speeding

VI. Miscellaneous

CHAPTER 5. FORENSIC ACCOUNTING

VI. Miscellaneous

CHAPTER 6. FORENSIC COMPUTER ANALYSIS

III. Trial Aids

IV. Miscellaneous

PART II. EVIDENCE BASED ON THE PHYSICAL SCIENCES

CHAPTER 7. FORENSIC DOCUMENT EXAMINATION

II. The Examination of Forensic–Related Documents

III. Evidence of Forensic Document Examinations

V.   Miscellaneous

CHAPTER 8.   FIREARM AND TOOLMARK IDENTIFICATION

III.   Principles of Firearms Identification

V.   Evidence of Firearm, Ammunition, and Toolmark Examinations

VIII.   Miscellaneous

CHAPTER 9.   FIRE SCENE AND EXPLOSIVES INVESTIGATION

II.   Basics of Fire Scene and Explosives Investigations

III.   Investigative Aspects

IV.   Laboratory Analysis

V.   Evidence of Fire Events and Explosives Use

VII.   Miscellaneous

CHAPTER 10.   FINGERPRINT IDENTIFICATION

I.   Introduction

CHAPTER 12. SPECTROGRAPHIC VOICE RECOGNITION

II. The Spectrographic Voice Recognition System

III. Evidence Of Voice Comparisons By Spectrograms

IV. Miscellaneous

CHAPTER 13. FORENSIC ACCIDENT RECONSTRUCTION

I. Introduction

II. The Investigation of Accidents

III. Legal Status Of Accident Reconstruction

IV. Miscellaneous

PART III. EXPERT TESTIMONY IN THE BIOLOGICAL AND LIFE SCIENCES

CHAPTER 14. FORENSIC PATHOLOGY

I. Introduction

CHAPTER 15. SEROLOGY AND TOXICOLOGY OF BODY FLUIDS

III. The Investigation Of Blood

CHAPTER 16. DRUGS AND THEIR CONTROL

IV. Evidential Status of Test Results

VI. Trial Aids

CHAPTER 17. FORENSIC DNA ANALYSIS— DETERMINING INDIVIDUALITY BY DNA

I. Introduction

IV. Evidentiary and Practical Aspects of DNA Analysis

CHAPTER 18. FORENSIC ODONTOLOGY

III. Evidence of Dental Identification

IV. Miscellaneous

CHAPTER 19. FORENSIC ANTHROPOLOGY

I. Introduction

II. Identification

PART IV.   BEHAVIORAL SCIENCE EVIDENCE

CHAPTER 20.   BEHAVIORAL SCIENCES AND THE LAW

I.   Introduction

III.   Forensic Psychiatry

IV.   Psychology and Law

V.   Forensic Neurology and Neuropsychology

VII.   Trial Practice

VIII.   Miscellaneous

CHAPTER 21.   EXPERT EVIDENCE ON INSANITY AND OTHER MENTAL HEALTH CONDITIONS

II.   The Defense of Insanity and Related Concepts

CHAPTER 22. EXPERT EVIDENCE ON WITNESS ACCURACY AND THE DETECTION OF DECEPTION

PART I—EYEWITNESSES AND MEMORY

II. The Issue of Trustworthiness of Eyewitness Recollection

III. Expert Evidence on the Accuracy of Child Witnesses

PART II—DETECTING DECEPTION

IV. The Polygraph Technique

**CHAPTER 23. BEHAVIORAL EVIDENCE IN PROCEED-
INGS INVOLVING CHILDREN AND FAMILIES**

II. Child Custody

TABLE OF CASES

Principal cases are in bold type. Non-principal cases are in roman type. References are to Pages.

2009 SUPPLEMENT

to

SCIENTIFIC EVIDENCE IN CIVIL AND CRIMINAL CASES

*

Part I

GENERAL CONCEPTS

Chapter 1

EXPERT EVIDENCE AND TESTIMONY

———

I. THE NATURE AND PURPOSE OF EXPERT EVIDENCE

§ 1.03 Tests of Admissibility

2. THE *FRYE* RULE—EXPERT TESTIMONY IN SEARCH OF A RATIONALE

Page 11. Update to footnote 7, *at the end of the footnote, add*:

In 2005, the Bureau of Justice Statistics, in its *Census of Publicly Funded Crime Laboratories* that existed in the United States at the end of 2002, determined that 351 such forensic crime laboratories existed. However, it was also found that not all forensic work is performed in these laboratories. "The other forensic work is done in police departments, sheriff's departments, and law enforcement agencies.... Typically the work is done in places called *identification units* or *fingerprint units* or *evidence units* or *crime-scene units*. These are not what you would think of as the traditional crime laboratory." Kristi Mayo, "The 'other' forensic scientists," quoting IAI chief operating officer in EVIDENCE TECHNOLOGY MAG., May–June, 2007, at 30. This included 203 state or regional laboratories, 65 county, 50 municipal and 33 federal laboratories.

See also, Jan Burke, "The State of American Crime Labs, 2006," FORENSIC MAG., Feb.–Mar. 2006 at 45.

4. *DAUBERT* INTERPRETS FEDERAL RULE OF EVIDENCE 702

Page 18. Update text, beginning on line 3 from the top of the page. *Insert the following additional paragraphs*:

A closer look at how the *Daubert* factors have been interpreted the courts shows that while the Supreme Court stressed that the listed factors were intended to furnish a "flexible" list of conditions to be explored, some of which might not universally apply to all forensic techniques, courts have rather routinely tested all techniques that were under challenge by whether they satisfied each one of the listed *Daubert* factors, and to what extent these "factors were said to be satisfied."[1]

1. Examples of this can be found in Chapters 7 on Forensic Document Examination, in § 7.17–4, listing post-*Daubert* decisions exploring the various factors in connection with an evaluation of handwriting comparison opinions, in Chapter 10 on

Yet, the "factors" mentioned do not necessarily provide a trustworthy guide in determining the reliability of conclusions reached by experts after analysis. Little needs to be added to discussion of the *General Acceptance Factor* that comes from the *Frye* decision. But some additional points ought to be considered when discussing the other *Daubert* factors.

The *Tested and Testability Factor* is supposedly a doctrine that comes to us from Austrian-born British philosopher of science Karl Popper's "falsifiability" or "refutability" criterion. The argument was first contained in Popper's German Language book first published in 1934.[2] In his later work *Conjectures* he "amplified that the demarcation between true science and pseudoscience is that scientific knowledge is based on falsifiable hypotheses that permit the inference (conclusion) to be drawn that, at least for the present, the underlying premises is probably true or probabilistically likely to be true."[3] But when Popper formulated his concept, he was not discussing crime laboratories or comparison sciences; he indeed used it in an attempt to discredit psychoanalysis and Marxism, both of which had at one time been postulated as based on scientific principles.

Nor has Popper's rule of falsifiability principle been uniformly accepted as the *best* description of science or scientific knowledge. Indeed, the principle has been soundly criticized as "as inadequate logical criterion" by scientist-lawyer Dr. Adina Schwartz,[4] and termed to be an "obsolete model of science" by Dr. Walter F. Rowe.[5] Despite the criticism, Popper's Falsifiability model provides a workable base line for judging whether a process provides reliable conclusions.

The *Peer Review and Publication* criterion fairs little better. The theory is that when a principle or methodology have been expounded on in published materials that have been scrutinized by subject specialists prior to publication, the publication provides a kind of seal of approval by the likely experts in the field and an objective assessment of its worth. If a method lacks reproducibility, in theory those who disagree with its trustworthiness will publish rebuttal articles. But that is by no means certain. Furthermore, an attempt to criticize a method may appear in a Letter to the Editor of a publication that is not indexed so as to be readily retrievable.

Editors also decide which articles to publish and which not to publish. Sometimes they succumb to outside pressures in either di-

---

Fingerprint Identification, in § 10.09–2 in connection with modern fingerprint comparison techniques, and in various other chapters dealing with comparison techniques.

2. Karl Popper, *Logik der Forschung,* 1934. In 1959, Basic Books, New York, published Popper's *The Logic of Scientific Discovery,* an updated translation of his earlier German text, and in 1962 Karl Popper's *Conjectures and Refutations: The Growth of*

Scientific Knowledge was printed. This latter volume was reprinted in 1968 by Harper and Row.

3. Andre Moenssens, article "Falsifiability Theory of Dr. Karl Popper," in WILEY ENCYCLOPEDIA OF FORENSIC SCIENCE, 2009.

4. See footnote 45 on page 23 of main text.

5. Id.

rection. In other cases, specialist reviewers who are asked to vet submitted articles may themselves disagree with an article yet recommend its publication because "the interesting though unvalidated approach" it may spark further commentary or suggest research to others in the profession.[6]

The *Error Rate Conundrum*. The measurement of error in applying a methodology is ordinarily used to determine the reliability of a result. It is most often seen as the statistical likelihood, expressed in fraction form, that a value calculated on the basis of multiple repeated experiments or collections of data correspond to its true value in a particular instance. The words can have a wide spectrum of meanings depending on the criteria used in its expression. Furthermore, different error rates may be calculated in the same discipline, depending on the question that is asked.

Typically, but not universally, a Type I error occurs when, in conducting comparisons, the result obtained is positive when in fact it should have been negative. That is termed a *false positive*. By contrast, where the result was negative even though the result should have been a positive one, this is called a Type II error or a *false negative*. These errors are primarily quantitative, that is, whether the result has some quality (such as being blood) or not.

The importance of determining what type of error was encountered will have a different relevancy depending on the factual issue that is sought to be resolved. Type I and Type II errors in methodology give information on two parameters of testing: the specificity and the sensitivity of a test. More sophisticated errors occur in quantitative analysis.[7]

After *Daubert*, the measurement of error in legal terms has acquired a quite distinct meaning from that which science awards it. *Daubert* suggested error rates are utilized determining the likelihood that a result obtained is "reliable." Yet, reliability has a very specific meaning in a scientific context that may differ from that in which lawyers may approach the term. In considering the reliability of a test result, it is important to know and understand the parameters; these should have been derived during the validation of the procedure. Each of these parameters can be a source of error.

Courts applying *Daubert* have had difficulties explaining exactly what is truly required when the term "error rate" is used.

Another significant misunderstanding of the *Daubert* error rate determination is that lawyers and courts have seen it as a measure of how often a particular examiner will reach an erroneous result (or its reverse, an accurate result.) Yet this misapplies the error rate concept of

---

6. For other comments on the *Daubert* factors, and the Peer Review factor in particular, see David W. Barnes, "General Acceptance Versus Scientific Soundness: Mad Scientists In the Courtroom," 31 FLA. STATE U. L. REV. 303, at 313 (2004), and other sources cited therein.

7. Much of the information is condensed from Moenssens, A.A., "Error Rates in Forensic Methods" in WILEY ENCYCLOPEDIA OF FORENSIC SCIENCE (Jamieson, A. & Moenssens, A.A., eds.) 2009 [1] 955.

Daubert. Calculation of an error rate presumes that the measurement will be done by appropriately trained and experienced examiners. *Daubert's* error has nothing to do with the individual conducting the test. And individuals misapplying the concept focus on the examiners, citing their performance on proficiency testing—or the absence of such tests—as a measure of their competence. That is not what *Daubert* was about. The accuracy of a result obtained by an individual examiner is a function of his or her qualifications to offer opinion evidence as an expert, not a measure of the appropriateness of the methodology used in the discipline.

Arguably, the most reliable—*cum* valid—criterion would be the existence of widely *Accepted Methodologies Demonstrating Validity* of a technique or test. The factor seeks to draw a little from all of the requirements discussed above but adds the all-important concepts of existing validation and quality control procedures. It also presumes the existence of appropriate interpretative measures, conflict resolution processes when workers in the field employed by one entity disagree, and adequate documentation that each step deemed necessary to an appropriate result has been scrupulously adhered to.

Page 27, at the end of subsection 6 on "Expert Opinions in the State Courts— Other Concerns and Considerations," *insert the following additional subsection*:

7. THE 2009 NATIONAL ACADEMY OF SCIENCE (NAS) REPORT STRENGTHENING FORENSIC SCIENCES IN THE UNITED STATES

a. INTRODUCTION

During the early 2000s, some forensic disciplines were criticized in law reviews and in court cases for lack of scientific rigor in the reaching of expert conclusions. This lack of rigor was spurred on by the United States Supreme Court decision in *Daubert,*[8] and the discovery that some comparative science disciplines had erroneously identified individuals as perpetrators of crimes which they were suspected to have committed. In some cases these misidentifications led to convictions. Largely through the efforts of the Innocence Project sponsored the Benjamin N. Cardozo School of Law and similar projects throughout the country, the occurrence of an alarming number of such erroneous convictions were exposed.

While in most of these cases convictions were influenced greatly by erroneous eyewitness identifications and by the use of suspect "snitch" testimony, ineffective lawyering in violation of a defendant's right to counsel, and the withholding by a prosecution of exculpatory evidence by the prosecution, in at least some cases deficient forensic testimony was

---

8. The standards for the admissibility of expert opinion evidence, including the various federal and state court decisions on the issue, are discussed extensively in Chapter 1 of the main text, as well as in other chapters where the issue was discussed.

said to have contributed to convictions. In many of these instances, additional forensic evidence, mainly DNA examinations, had brought to light the misidentifications. While the extent to which examiner testimony contributed to or caused erroneous convictions cannot be definitively established in all cases, the very occurrence of analytical mistakes caused a great concern among many who believed the *Daubert* and *Kumho Tire* decisions of the United States Supreme Court[9] had been interpreted by lower courts in an insufficiently rigorous fashion. Others suggested the Court's decisions were themselves part of the blame for failing to provide clearer guidelines for the use of expert opinion evidence.

In 2006, under a new Act, Congress authorized the National Academy of Sciences to study the various practices involved in forensic science services in the country. The mandate was broad based, requiring the study to focus on a lot of aspects of forensic science, beginning with evidence collection through examination and use of analytical results as courtroom testimony, and culminating in assessing the present and future needs of forensic science and making recommendations for the future. A Committee was appointed by NAS in the fall of 2006 to implement the congressional mandate.

The Committee was composed of members of academia, forensic science communities, lawyers, judges and scientists. Its project would have as its main purpose: "Identifying the Needs of the Forensic Science Community." Eight meetings were held throughout 2007 and 2008, at which experts from all sectors of the various evidence examination disciplines were invited to make presentations. The presenters included law enforcement officials, scientists, medical examiners, crime laboratory personnel, defense attorneys, law professors and other academics, private practitioners in forensic science, educators, and representatives of relevant professional organizations.

The long-awaited Report (hereinafter NAS Report) was publicly revealed on February 18, 2009.[10] Prior to its publication, some press reports had characterized the NAS Report as condemning crime laboratories for using techniques that lacked science. When the Report became available, it confirmed some of the alarming findings that forensic scientists already had anticipated and raised additional ones. The reaction of the forensic science communities was generally supportive of the need for more research and for the Report's recognition that forensic science services are grossly underfunded. Neither of these two points came as any surprise. The need for additional research, which has been long overdue in some specific disciplines, has not only been recognized after *Daubert* challenges began to be made, but had already spurred some ground-breaking new research on many fronts. Research, however, is time-intensive and therefore costly. The recognition that additional funding for research is a requirement if the delivery of reliable forensic

---

9. See, supra § 1.03(4) and (4).

10. Its Executive Summary became available at that moment free of charge at http://www.nap.edu. The full Report, protected by copyright, was to be available for purchase from the National Academies.

services is to be guaranteed has long been a serious budgetary problem for scientific evidence disciplines.

b. An Overview of the Report's Principal Findings

The Report overall appears to exhibit a general distrust of crime laboratories and publicly-supported laboratories because they are seen as being associated with and beholden to the prosecution in criminal cases. This connection also suggests the possibility of bias of examiners or laboratories leading to faulty forensic results. To justify that distrust, the Report relies heavily on writings by defense attorneys, academics and law professors who are not themselves forensic scientists but who have long been critical of the forensic science services. The arguments are sought to be bolstered by references to a few widely publicized instances where miscarriages of justice are reported to have occurred. That it was shown to have occurred in a several different forensic disciplines and services did not enhance the trust in the delivery of forensic services overall.[11] The public clamor that resulted from some widely publicized attributions of incriminating evidence to accused individuals who were later shown to lack the connection to the evidence upon which the prosecution relied as proof of guilt as well as the temporary closing of several forensic laboratories in several states where errors were said to have occurred provides considerable justification for that mistrust.[12]

This led the Committee's members to conclude that crime laboratories and medical investigators place an over-reliance on expert witness testimony that is not based on scientifically validated methodologies; that these expert witnesses in at least some of the disciplines are largely untrained in scientific methods; are susceptible to pro-prosecution bias; and lack adequate training, education, and certification. This was found to be more the case in those disciplines that have long been accepted uncritically by courts wherein its practitioners seek to individualize certain types of evidence as having a "positive" connection to a suspect. These disciplines are sometimes referred to inartfully as "comparative science" methods. The examiners sometimes justified their conclusions on the basis of some mantra such as "nature never duplicates itself," or "no two snowflakes are alike," and "everything in nature is different," whether or not these proffered justifications can be shown to apply to specific forms of evidence.

As a result of that finding by the Committee, the Report presents us with some very drastic recommendations, of which perhaps the most far-reaching one is the creation of a brand new and independent federal

---

11. See NAS Report, Chapters 1 through 7.

12. The NAS Report, on pp. I-8 & 9, singles out repeatedly the erroneous accusation by leading FBI experts of Brandon Mayfield as the person whose latent fingerprint was associated with the Madrid, Spain, train bombing as having been caused by institutional bias. The Report also mentions the frauds of the late West Virginia State Police Crime Laboratory expert Fred Zain in the early 1990s, suspected bitemark cases, and the closing of sections of the crime laboratory in Houston, Texas.

agency in which all forensic analyses that may result in evidence in criminal prosecutions—and presumably civil trials as well[13]—will be conducted pursuant to scientifically validated methodologies by science-trained examiners who have been certified to be competent in their specialties. The facts that many crime laboratories are accredited by a self-policing association of their directors,[14] and that in many forensic fields more or less rigorous certifications are already in place, failed to assuage the concerns of the Committee in light of the few widely publicized cases of erroneous attributions that had occurred in disciplines where its experts were considered to be professionals who had been "certified" as competent. These experts had professed to near absolute certainty in reaching their conclusions, and yet their opinions were shown to have been in error.[15]

The Report's recommendation further seeks to affect the manner in which an expert's conclusions are to be reported to courts and users of forensic results. It indicated a clear preference for statistically validated assertions of the likelihood that a methodology will provide consistently reliable conclusions.

It was further recommended that expert reports be more explicit in identifying the types of examinations conducted and that are available in a science. A careful documentation of the various steps used in the analysis process should be made as well. Such documentation would have to be provided along with the report, and should also include all contemporaneous "bench notes" made during the process.[16]

The Report finds similar deficiencies in the medico-legal investigation of death and recommends that jurisdictions do away with antiquated coroner systems wherein such investigations are largely conducted by medically untrained or insufficiently trained examiners, some of whom may be elected. The modern medical examiner system, which is required in many states, should become the model for the investigation of death, the Report recommends.

Recommendations also include setting standards for forensic education, training, accreditation, and continuing education in all disciplines where examinations are likely to result in the giving of expert opinion evidence.

Almost as an afterthought, the Report further provides a brief chapter on automated fingerprint identification systems to remedy inter-

---

13. The Federal Rules of Evidence on expert opinion testimony apply to civil as well as criminal cases.

14. ASCLAD–LAB: The Association of Crime Laboratory Directors—Laboratory Accreditation Board.

15. The NAS Report, on p. 5–12, singles out the fact that "fingerprint examiners typically testify in the language of absolute certainty," and make the claim "that they have matched the latent print to the one and only person in the entire world whose fingertip could have produced it." Such a conclusion was not only deemed to be "unjustified," but also scientifically insupportable. See further comments on that issue in Chapter 10 of this Supplement.

16. NAS Report, Chapters 6 and 7. It should be noted that this practice is already recommended or required in many forensic disciplines by the existing Quality Assurance. Standards.

operatibility challenges,[17] and on the role forensic science and biometrics are to play in Homeland Security.[18] The Report concludes with two appendices giving biographies of its committee members and staff, as well as the agendas and names of the persons who testified at the Committee's five meetings during 2007.

Most of the Report's chapters will be discussed in more detail in this Chapter or in other Chapters of this Supplement.

Despite incorrect media hype and overreaction by some, it is important to stress what the NAS Report does ***not*** contain. The following excerpt of the Statement made by Kenneth E. Melson, Acting Director of the Bureau of Alcohol, Tobacco, Firearms and Explosives, and a former President of the American Academy of Forensic Science deals with the issuer:

> "... The report does not, and was never intended to, comprehensively assess the forensic sciences themselves.... Likewise, the report does not undermine the use of forensic science generally—or any specific discipline—in the courtroom. As one of the co-chairs of the report committee put it, 'the question of whether forensic evidence in a particular case is admissible under applicable law is not coterminus with the question whether there are studies confirming the scientific validity and reliability of a forensic science discipline.' Further, the report does not, and was never intended to, offer any judgments on any cases currently in the judicial system. Finally, the report does not recommend any rule or law changes in the area of evidentiary admissibility ... In sum, DOJ views the report as a positive contribution to a critical debate, but it should be considered in the appropriate context."[19]

Elsewhere, Acting Director Melson, who suggested the Department of Justice supports "virtually all of the recommendations," emphasized the significant strides that have already been made in regard to many recommendations. He also stresses:

> The report rightly acknowledges the important contributions that forensic science has made to the criminal justice system, both in convicting the guilty and exonerating the innocent. As Judge Harry Edwards stated, "The work of the forensic science community is critically important in our system of criminal justice."[20]

Lest the report be misunderstood, Melson stated:

> Indeed, the report does not, and was not intended to be, a full-scale review of the state of each discipline. Rather, the report summarizes a portion of the current knowledge about the disciplines, but does not recount in detail the full scope of the science that has been done

---

17. NAS Report, Chapter 10.

18. NAS Report, Chapter 11.

   19. Kenneth E. Melson, Statement before the House of Representatives Committee on the Judiciary, Subcommittee on

Crime, Terrorism, and Homeland Security, presented on May 13, 2009, on behalf of the Department of Justice.

   20. Id.

on each. If the report had included a more comprehensive review of the literature, it could have cited a wealth of published, peer-reviewed research that demonstrates the rigor of particular scientific methods when applied in a forensic context. (The FBI Lab is in the process of publishing such a review for each of the disciplines). After all, it would be difficult to do so in the case of, for example, fingerprint analysis, a discipline that has more than 100–year history of use in law enforcement but is addressed in only six and a half pages in the report. There is a vast amount of research that validates the use of latent fingerprints that was not cited by the report....[21]

c.   The NAS Report—Creating a New Agency Recommended

After an introductory chapter on what comprises the "forensic science" and the pressures such as case backlog, insufficient resources, the growth of the new standard in forensics set by the development of forensic DNA technology, Chapter 1 of the Report begin its questioning of the legitimacy of some methodologies which are prone to produce errors and fraud because of claimed lack of validation or use of questionable science.[22]

In Chapter 2, the Report begins in earnest its criticism of existing forensic practices and of the weaknesses in the current structure of its supporting organizations. After analyzing the service providers, case backlog, and forensic services provided by crime laboratory associated departments,[23] the Report analyzes current service providers to lead up to its first recommendation which calls for "a more central, strategic, and integrated approach to forensic science at the national level."[24] This leads in to perhaps the most revolutionary recommendation for change from current forensic evidentiary practices: the creation new Agency, called a National Institute of Forensic Science (NIFS), to be created by federal law.

The new NIFS would be independent, and remove from law enforcement control or prosecution affiliation all analytical functions of scientific evidence to be used in criminal litigation. Other than simply proposing this new agency, the Report provides little guidance on how this would work, given the mammoth-sized existing forensic science establishments, in a practical and highly politically charged system. The Report simply conclude it is needed, and then spells out everything that this new agency would be required to achieve.

---

21.   Ibid.

22.   Relying on documentation provided by the Innocence Project, and while recognizing that, in the overall volume of criminal prosecutions, the instances of errors reported are probably rare occurrences, the Report mentions, on pp. I–8 through I–10, laboratory mishandling and mislabeling, falsification of results, "drylabbing," misinterpretation, suppression of exculpatory evidence, and exaggerations of the significance of findings, as well as bias, as causes for its mistrust.

23.   On p. 2–7 The Report cites a study reporting that two-thirds of fingerprint identifications take place "outside of traditional crime laboratories."

24.   NAS Report, p. 2–1.

Recommendation No. 1 provides:

> To promote development of forensic science into a mature field of multidisciplinary research and practice, founded on the systematic condition and analysis of relevant data, Congress should establish and appropriate funds for an independent federal entity, the National Institute of Forensic Science (NIFS). NIFS should have a full-time administrator and an advisory board with expertise in research and education, the forensic science disciplines, physical and life sciences, forensic pathology, engineering, information technology, measurements and standards, testing ane evaluation, national security, and public policy. . . .[25]

The recommendation goes on to suggest that the NIFS should have a broad mandate: (1) to establish and enforce best practices for both examiners and laboratories; (2) require mandatory accreditation of laboratories furnishing forensic services as well as require mandatory certification for forensic science professionals and medical examiners.[26]

The recommendation continues with a variety of other ancillary tasks of the NIFS in promoting competitive and peer-reviewed research, developing strategies to improve research and education, funding state and local agencies in research projects and funding, and policing education policies. Perhaps recognizing that this ambitious and costly new creation is unlikely to occur, the chapter concludes with the admonition that each of the Report's individual recommendations stands on its own. Even if this grand proposition does not come to fruition, "the committee vigorously supports the adoption of the core ideas and principles embedded in the additional recommendations that appear in this report."[27]

The creation of yet another federal agency, and its attendant lagtime in operational readiness, would not only be costly, but "unnecessarily duplicative of well-established programs now found within several federal agencies,"according to John W. Hicks, Director of the Northeast Regional Forensic Institute at the State University of New York at Albany.[28]

Chapter 3 of the Report contains mainly an analysis of legal developments in forensic evidence, beginning with *Frye v. United States* through the advent of the Federal Rules of Evidence and *Daubert v. Merrell Dow Pharmaceuticals* and it's progeny.[29] These discussions on law, already covered in the main text of this book, are not summarized here.

The point that is stressed here, however, is that the Committee found little support in science for "individualization" testimony offered in fingerprint, firearm and toolmark identification, bitemark, and some trace evidence opinions. It stated, in this regard:

25. NAS Report. p. 2–21.

26. Id.

27. NAS Report, p. 2–22.

28. Statement of John W. Hicks before the U.S. House of Representatives Committee of the Judiciary, Subcommittee on Crime, Terrorism, and Homeland Security, on May 13, 2009.

29. See Chapter 1 of main text, at pp. 1–27.

As discussed in Chapters 4 and 5, no forensic method other than nuclear DNA analysis has been rigorously shown to have the capacity to consistently and with a high degree of certainty, support conclusions about "individualization" (more commonly known as "matching" of an unknown item of evidence to a specific known source). In terms of scientific basis, the analytically based disciplines generally hold a notable edge over discipline based on expert interpretation.[30]

After analyzing the *Daubert* case and its successor cases, the Report examined how the Supreme Court's new approach—to require scientific reliability—has been applied in the lower and appeals courts, illustrating its discussion with brief references, successively to DNA, drug identification, fingerprints, firearm and toolmark cases, as well as references to bitemark cases. The Report's approach to these disciplines is discussed in this Supplement in the appropriate chapters that correspond to their topics.

The chapter concludes by admonishing that "Law enforcement officials and the members of society they serve need to be assured that forensic techniques are *reliable*."[31] This rejoinder serves as the introduction to Chapter 4 which explores the principles of scientific inquiry and the interpretation of scientific data.

While there is no single definition as to what is understood by the "scientific method," but rather a compilation of descriptions that are said to support reliable data analysis, all of the definitions adopted in groups ultimately stress that progress in scientific knowledge comes as a result of the accumulation and study of data wherein strengths and weaknesses of information are assessed, as a result of which repeatable results in using a given method may be predicted The chapter discusses the various approaches that science generally recognizes as "valid" in advancing knowledge. Research, the accumulation of data, its analysis in light of hypotheses that are tested, ultimately may lead to results that then need to be further validated. The process was described in the main text of this book at p. 13–15.

Chapter 4 recognizes that the scientific process is subject to uncertainty and a variety of potential sources of error, the importance of which it is crucial to keep into account in formulating an opinion that purports to estimate the probative value of a specific item of evidence in a given case. Significant space was allotted to a discussion of "the error rate," which is one of the factors that *Daubert* identified as affecting the "reliability" (probative value) of evidence. An error rate, is defined as the "proportion of cases in which the analysis led to a false conclu-

30. NAS Report, pp. 3–2 & 3. The Report recognized in the immediately following paragraph that there are more established protocols and available research for the analysis of fingerprints than for bitemark comparisons, cautioning, however, that not all evidence is equally valuable because much depends on the quality of the latent fingerprint image.

31. NAS Report, p. 3–19.

sion.''[32] Though very little validated research on the issue, Chapter 4 further alerts the reader to the possibility that human judgment may be significantly affected by bias and expectations, whether conscious or subconscious, of an examiner.[33]

The chapter concludes with what is essentially a reiteration of the Supreme Court's admonitions in *Daubert* about the need to insure reliability in the scientific enterprise through careful hypothesis testing, validation studies, error rate studies, and peer reviewed publications. The need for periodic reevaluation of what has become accepted as appropriate remains is also stressed as a necessity. The Report stated, ''The premium that science places on precision, objectivity, critical thinking, careful observation and practice, repeatability, uncertainty management, and peer review enables the reliable collection, measurement, and interpretation of clues in order to produce knowledge.''[34]

d. SOME TRADITIONAL FORENSIC SCIENCES COME UNDER FIRE

In Chapter 5, at 42 pages the longest of all chapters, as well as in Chapter 6, the Report analyzes the strengths and weaknesses of several forensic science disciplines. While recognizing that some of the well established evidence evaluations of crime laboratories are based on solid scientific principles and are supported by solid bases of theory and research,[35] ''many other technique,'' the Report asserts

> have been developed heuristically. That is, they are based on observation, experience, and reasoning without an underlying scientific theory, experiments designed to test the uncertainties and reliability of method, or sufficient data that are collected and analyzed scientifically.[36]

(i) The DNA "standard"—Is it to be the model for all forensic sciences?

Going back to the solid theory-based practices, the analysis of many forms of biological evidence has culminated in the development of forensic DNA analysis. The Report concludes that the various current DNA techniques, which are discussed in the chapter, in the form of laboratory analytical methods of evidence examination leading to conclusions of which an error rate can be calculated statistically, are to be held out as the standard against which many other forensic individualization techniques are to be measured.

32. NAS Report, at pp. 4–7 & 8. See also this Supplement's discussion or Daubert's ''error rate'' factor on page 3, supra.

33. NAS Report, p. 4–10, referring to anecdotal evidence: the example of the Brandon Mayfield case which will be discussed in more detail in the Supplement to Chapter 10.

34. NAS Report, p. 4–11.

35. The Report mentions DNA analysis, serology, forensic pathology, toxicology, chemical analysis, and digital and multimedia forensics.

36. NAS Report, p. 5–1.

The chapter also evaluates the analysis of controlled substances as well as the weaknesses in reporting laboratory results in too "terse" a fashion.[37]

(ii) Comparing DNA standard to the methods that rely on observation and comparison

The next almost seven pages of the Report's Chapter 5 are devoted to an extensive critique of friction ridge analysis (fingerprints) techniques.[38] Despite over 100 years of court acceptance worldwide, this most venerable of the forensic methods, which at one time was called "the gold standard" against which all forensic techniques ought to be compared, came in for some very serious criticism, at least when it came to comparing unknown crime scene impressions to known prints. While recognizing that exclusions could often be reliably made expeditiously, the methods of "matching" several prints to the same source and the manner of expressing conclusion came under severe fire.

Apart from discussion of fingerprints in Chapter 5, there is also a separate Chapter 10 connected to the same topic. That chapter discusses the interoperability problems which arise in the use of Automatic Fingerprint Identification Systems (AFIS). Since this topic is related to the fingerprint identification discussion in the Report's Chapter 5, and because of the broad-brush nature of the its treatment of these topics, the Report's comments on fingerprints will be analyzed separately in some detail in the appropriate chapter of this Supplement.[39]

The next category of impression evidence in Chapter 5 of the NAS Report is shoeprints and tire impressions.[40] Four pages are devoted to these two techniques. The import of the Report's discussion on these topics will also be included later in this Supplement the discussion of the topic of Trace Evidence.

Toolmark and firearm identification are the next topics discussed in Chapter 5 of the NAS Report.[41] In its evaluation of the methods used and conclusions reached, the NAS Report echoed many of the concerns it had expressed with regard to fingerprints and other impression evidence. The NAS Report observations and findings of this chapter are separately analyzed and discussed in the 2009 Supplement to Chapter 8 of the main text.

A like treatment will be reserved for the NAS Report on hair and fiber evidence,[42] which is the next topic of chapter 5 of the NAS Report, as well as forensic document analysis,[43] paint analysis,[44] explosives

---

37. NAS Report, pp. 5–2 through 5–7. See, in this regard, Chapters 15, 16, and 17 of the main text wherein these subjects are the main concern.

38. NAS Report, p. 5–7.

39. The subject of friction ridge analysis is dealt with in Chapter 10 of the main text (fifth edition) and a discussion of the NAS Report's conclusions will therefore be dealt with in this Supplement in the same Chapter 10 treatment, infra.

40. NAS Report, p. 5–14. See, infra, this Supplement under Chapter 11.

41. NAS Report, p. 5–18. See, infra, this Supplement under Chapter 8.

42. NAS Report, p. 5–22. See, infra, this Supplement under Chapter 11.

43. NAS Report, p. 5–27. See, infra, this Supplement under Chapter 11.

44. NAS Report, p. 5–30. See, infra, this Supplement under Chapter 11.

evidence,[45] odontology (especially bitemarks),[46] and bloodstain pattern analysis.[47]

The NAS Report's chapter 5, at p. 5–39, concludes with a discussion of a newly emerging and already widely recognized discipline of digital and multimedia analysis. Unlike other forensic disciplines, the Report only spends scant space at evaluating the potentiality or ought (including the reliability) of what the discipline purports to achieve.

(iii) The impediments to reliability

The discussion in Chapter 6 of the Report is but a continuation of the critical assessment of the impression evidence methods dealt with in the previous chapter. It also continues to stress the need for empirical research which has long been lacking. This need has been recognized by forensic scientists generally for decades, but the lack of uniformity of approaches has yet to result in a consensus on any issue within the forensic science community. Research has been approached in a piece-meal fashion by interested practitioners who sought to engage in specific projects as time and resources permitted. It is in this area where a well-funded and staffed independent entity as the recommended National Institute of Forensic Science (NIFS), discussed earlier, could perhaps make its greatest contribution to improving the delivery of forensic services. There are other avenues of federal funding for useful and desirable research projects to be carried on in universities, acting in cooperation with crime laboratory specialists as the sources of data.

After discussing the dependence of forensic laboratories on law enforcement agencies, and the attendant budgetary problems in allocation of resources—long lamented by these laboratories which have been and are chronically underfunded and understaffed—as well as the potential for bias that such a dependence ;promotes, the chapter continues by focusing on the level of uncertainty with which experts have delivered their findings and conclusions in lab reports and court testimony.

Chapter 6 concludes by the presentation of Recommendations Nos. 2, 3, 4 and 5.

In Recommendation #2, the Report would charge the proposed NIFS with establishing standards with regard to the terminology with which examiners should report on and testify about their examination results. It is further recommended that NIFS establish model laboratory report for each discipline, specifying the minimum amount of information about each analysis or investigation that should be included in a report. The use of these standards should be mandatory for the accreditation and certification processes.

Recommendation #3 emphasizes the need for research "to address issues of accuracy, reliability, and validity in the forensic science disci-

---

45. NAS Report, p. 5–33. See, infra, this Supplement under Chapter 8.

46. NAS Report, p. 5–35. See, infra, this Supplement under Chapter 18.

47. NAS Report, p. 5–38. See, infra, this Supplement under Chapter 15.

plines.''[48] The onus for funding of competitive peer-reviewed research is placed on the proposed NIFS, and encompasses nor only the establishing of a scientific basis for demonstrating the reliability of methods, but also practically-oriented assessments of forensic techniques in real-life scenarios that are averaged across a representative group of examiners and laboratories. It is also expected that the research would develop quantifiable measures of uncertainty in expert conclusions as well as automated techniques to enhance technologies.

Recommendation #4 invites Congress to appropriate the necessary funds to NIFS so that all state and local forensic laboratories can be removed from the administrative control of law enforcement and the prosecution function.

Following on previously discussed issues, the final Recommendation #5 of Chapter 6 entreats the NIFS to encourage research on human observer bias and sources of human error in forensic examinations. These studies in the various types of bias, including contextual bias, should ultimately lead to standard protocols developed by NIFS by which bias and human error can be minimized to the greatest extent possible.

e.   Strengthening Oversight Through Laboratory Accreditation

Chapter 7 of the NAS Report[49] is concerned with the fact that there are currently few requirements for the accreditation of laboratories of forensic science. While such regulations exist in some state with respect to clinical laboratories, the chapter recognizes that if persons decide to open a forensic laboratory, they can do so currently without needing to satisfy accreditation standards or subject themselves to quality assurance measures in all but three (New York, Oklahoma, and Texas) states. Limited progress has been made through the voluntary participation on some accrediting programs initiated by concerned groups, but nothing compels a laboratory to seek this accreditation.

After describing in detail the requirements and operations of the existing voluntary participation programs of several organizations, primarily the American Society of Crime Laboratory Directors, Laboratory Accreditation Board (ASCLD/LAB), incorporated not for profit in 1988. Thereafter, the group established another separate entity in 1995 charged with training, education and support of accreditation. That group is the National Forensic Science Technology Center (NFSTC). ASCLD/LAB subsequently required that ISO/IEC 17025 international standard for testing and calibrating laboratories[50] become the norm. Accreditations under this standard were approved beginning in 2003. The program is a rigorous one, and focuses on all aspects of laboratory operations.

---

48. NAS Report, p. 6–6.

49. NAS Report, pp. 7–1 through 7–17.

50. See www.iso.org/iso/catalogue_detail?csnumber=39883.

While a significant percentage of publicly funded laboratories have sought voluntary accreditation,[51] only a few jurisdiction mandate that forensic laboratories seek accreditation. The delivery of many forensic services, however, is not offered by forensic laboratories, but instead by specialist groups that operate as units independent of an all-service forensic laboratory. Primary among them are identification bureaus of law enforcement agencies where, according to the International Association for Identification (IAI) the bulk of all fingerprint comparison and much trace evidence analysis as well as firearm and toolmark comparison is performed.

The chapter also discusses the groups which set standards for use in a variety of forensic disciplines. The best known among them is the American Society for Testing and Materials International (ASTM). This group has established standards in the forensic document examination field, discussed in Chapter 7 of the Fifth of the main text. ASTM also has developed a standard guide for forensic paint analysis and comparison, for the non-destructive examination of paper, for the forensic analysis of fibers by infrared spectroscopy, and the standard terminology for expressing conclusions of forensic document examiners.

Some federal institutions are also active in the same pursuit. The National Institute of Standards and Technology (NIST) is a research organization publishing standard in a few forensic fields, notably in organic gunshot residue analysis, trace explosives detectors, and improvised explosive devices.

With the support and financing of the FBI, a series of specialized Scientific Working Groups (SWGs) are active in a variety of forensic disciplines. At this times SWGs exist for the firearm and toolmark examiners (SWGGUN), forensic document examiners (SWGDOC), materials analysis (SWGMAT), bloodstain pattern analysis (SWGSTAIN), DNA analysis methods (SWGDAM), dog and orthogonal detector guidelins (SWGDOG), forensic analysis of chemical terrorism (SWGFACT), forensic analysis of radiological materials (SWGFARM), friction ridge analysis, study and technology (SWGFAST), microbial genetics and forensics (SWGMGF), and shoeprint and tire tread evidence (SWGTREAD). A separate SWG is sponsored by the Drug Enforcement Administration for the analysis of seized drugs (SWGDRUG). Each one of these groups maintains its own website on which its workings can be monitored. All of these SWGs are either developing guidelines or standards for their constituent groups

The National Academy of Science found that the impact of these SWGs and other standard-setting groups was difficult to measure, since most, if not all, rely on voluntary adherence to their standards and guidelines, and lack adequate enforcement mechanisms. Further, the standards promulgated by one group may be different from other organi-

---

51. According to Kenneth Melson's statement before a subcommittee of the U.S. House of Representatives on May 13, 2009, referenced supra on p. 8 of this Supplement, 97% of publicly funded laboratories are fully accredited.

zations seeking to guide the same group of professionals, or by those set independently by individual laboratories.

Proficiency testing of the laboratory functions is an essential component of a proper quality assurance program. But such programs as already exist were also found by NAS to be insufficiently rigorous. The practices currently used were analyzed in the chapter.[52]

The NAS review of existing examiner competency peer certification programs was equally unsatisfactory in the Academy's view. The programs of various organizationally-sponsored certification programs were also discussed in the chapter in some detail, along with the federal Justice for All Act of 2004 which created Coverdale Forensic Science Improvements Grants. Despite the existence of a great variety of certification programs, the NAS was not convinced that adequate oversight existed or that the sponsoring groups' requirement were sufficiently rigorous to guarantee adequate examiner competence in many fields. Even so, participation in certification examinations was not mandatory to exercising professional duties in forensic science.

Belonging to a professional association which requires its members to adhere to a Code of Ethics is believed to be some guarantee of competence and/or honesty. Most forensic membership organizations maintain Ethics Committees. While the Codes of Ethics proscribe certain conduct on pain of professional sanctions, they differ widely in what is considered to be acceptable conduct. Also, the NAS Report found them to be conflicting in their terms, and inconsistent in their enforcement. No uniform code of ethics in the forensic professions exists.

In view of all of these haphazard approaches to accreditation, quality assurance programs, competency assessment and examiner certification, the NAS concludes its Chapter 7 with four additional recommendations:

Recommendation #6 urges Congress to allocate funds to NIFS to develop tools for validating forensic methodologies and develop standards for adequate practice in each discipline, with the cooperation of NIST, the Scientific Working Groups of the FBI, government laboratories, universities, and private laboratories. After standards that reflect best practices are developed for each discipline, the documents should serve as accrediting tools and guides for education and certification.

Recommendation #7 suggests that laboratory accreditation and examiner certification should be mandatory for all forensic science professionals. The standards to be applies should be compatible with those of recognized international groups such as ISA. After a specific time period to be established by NIFS has elapsed, no professional would be permitted to testify in court without an appropriate certification awarded after written examination, supervised practice, proficiency testing, continuing education, recertification procedures, adherence to a code of ethics, and subject to effective disciplinary procedures.

---

52. NAS Report, p. 7–12.

Recommendation #8 reiterates some of what is evident from previous discussions. All forensic laboratories must establish effective routine quality assurance and quality control procedures, so that error and bias can be minimized.

The final recommendation (Recommendation #9) requires NIFS to establish a national code of ethics for all disciplines, recommend individual societies to incorporate this code in their own organizational documents, and further explore the mechanisms whereby serious ethical misconduct by an individual can be sanctioned. The code is to be enforced through the certification process, which means, presumably, that the finding of the commission of a serious ethical violation will result in loss of accreditation.

As a corollary of its concerns over certification and accreditation, Chapter 8 of the NAS Report examines the education and training in the forensic sciences. Recognizing that forensic science has seen a proliferation of forensic education programs despite the fact that no doctoral level (PhD) educational opportunities are offered in forensic science at colleges or universities, the chapter examines in some detail all of the existing approaches.[53] Predictably, the chapter ends with Recommendation #10 charging the proposed NIFS to develop graduate level educational programs in forensic science, as well as continuing legal education programs in law schools for law students, legal practitioners, and judges.

f.   THE MEDICO-LEGAL INVESTIGATION OF DEATH

In Chapter 9, the NAS Report takes on the still widely used though anachronistic coroner system of death investigation. Coroners have been charged with this function since the middle ages. Coroners are typically elected individuals who need not satisfy medical educational requirements in some jurisdictions and who wield significant electoral power in many states.

It deserves mention at this early stage that doing away with the coroner system, which is a constitutionally mandated office in some States, may present perhaps the greatest hurdle to adoption of the chapter's final recommendation.#11, which suggest requiring that all medico-legal investigations of death are conducted by qualified medical examiners who are board certified in forensic pathology. The 21 pages of this Chapter are discussed separately in this Supplement's Chapter 14, infra, on Forensic Pathology.

g.   CONCLUSION

Chapter 10, as mentioned supra, deals with Automated Fingerprint Identification System interoperability problems, and is discussed separate in Chapter 10 of this Supplement, infra, discussing fingerprint identification.

---

53.   NAS Report, pp. 8–1 through 8–18.

Chapter 11, the concluding chapter of the NAS Report, is titled Homeland Security and the Forensic Science Disciplines. It reviews, in five brief pages, the current approaches to research and the dangers to the United States in these perilous times where crime is significantly internationalized. It recognizes the current efforts of the FBI, the Department of Defense's (DOD) Army Criminal Investigation Laboratory, the Cyber Crime Center, the DNA laboratories, the Center for Disease Control, the Biometrics Task Force of DOD, the National Biodefense Forensic Analysis Center, the Office of the Director of National Intelligence in the fight to defend the United States.

These discussions lead to the predictable final recommendation of the report that these tasks be coordinated in some fashion by its proposed NIFS so that evidence from events that affect national security can be adequately preserved.

––––––

IV. DISCOVERY AND DISCLOSURE IN CIVIL CASES

§ 1.18   The 2006 E–Discovery Amendments—The Day of ESI (Electronically Stored Information) is here

Page 70, at the end of line 8 (also the end of the paragraph), *insert the following new footnote*:

The obligations of counsel in respect of hitherto unknown aspects of E–Discovery have featured at many trial bar seminars and in many practice-oriented legal publications. In 2007, the American Bar Association's THE SCITECH LAWYER (Vol.4, Issue 2, Fall 2007) published an entire issue devoted to *DISCOVERY—ALL THINGS ELECTRONIC,* edited by Eleanor B. Kellett. The issue include the following articles:

—Douglas W. Kim, "A–Discovery: A Practical Approach," at p. 6.

—Sarah Michaels Montgomery, "E–Discovery: Aligning Practice with Principles," at p. 12.

—Andrew Bowden, "E–Discovery Challenges and Technologies," at p. 16.

—Steven W. Teppler, "Spoliation of Digital Evidence: A Changing Approach to Challenges and Sanctions," at p. 20, and other items.

See also, Jason Krause, *"Rockin' Out The E–Law,"* ABA JOURNAL, July 2008, p. 48; Shira A Scheindlin & Jonathan M. Redgrave, "E–Discovery: Technology requires greater car in preserving evidence," ABA JOURNAL, April 2008, p. 26.

While court decisions on e-Discovery have been popping up left and right, Dean Gonsowski, on December 12, 2008, published "Top 5 Cases That Shaped Electronic Discovery in 2008" at http://www.clearwell systems.com/e-discovery-blog/22008/12/12/ top–5–cases ..., visited on Dec. 19, 2008.

––––––

VI. THE EXPERT AT TRIAL

§ 1.21 Direct Examination

2. LEGAL IMPEDIMENTS TO EXPERT TESTIMONY

b. HEARSAY

Page 85. Addition to footnote 14, *at the end of the existing footnote 14, add*:

The United States Supreme Court recently granted *certiorari* in Commonwealth v. Melendez–Diaz, 69 Mass.App.Ct. 1114, 870 N.E.2d 676 (2007), cert. granted —— U.S. ——, 128 S.Ct. 1647 (2008), to review whether a state forensic analyst's laboratory report that has been prepared for use in a criminal prosecution I "testimonial" evidence and thus subject to Confrontation Clause restrictions detailed in Crawford v. Washington, supra.

Page 86. Addition of a new footnote. *At the end of the second full paragraph of page 86, add the following new footnote*:

16a. Whether *Crawford*'s constitutional requirement applies to the admission of laboratory reports under FRE 803(6) is currently undecided. Lower court decisions are in conflict. See, in this regard, the detailed examination of the issue in Edward J. Imwinkelried, " 'This is like déjà vu all over again': The Third Constitutional Attack on the Admissibility of Police Laboratory Reports in Criminal Cases," 38 N.M. L.Rev. 303 (2008).

§ 1.22 Cross–Examination

2. IMPEACHMENT OF THE EXPERT

Page 95, at the end of the section, and before § 1.23, *insert the following additional subsection*:

3. EXPOSING MISTAKES IN EXPERT OPINIONS AND DECEPTIVE OR FRAUDULENT EXPERTS

Recent literature in forensic science has exposed that a number of errors have been committed in casework by forensic scientists that were not caught prior to their testimony in civil and criminal cases. The errors that have gained the most attention national are those that have been exposed as resulting in wrongful convictions, primarily, though not exclusively, through the efforts of the Innocence Project developed by Peter Neufeld and Barry C. Scheck at the Benjamin N. Cardozo School of Law. Mention has been made of this earlier in this chapter, and it is a problem that is also alluded to in several chapters dealing with specific techniques.

See also the studies by Marvin Zalman, Brad Smith and Angie Kiger, published as "Officials' Estimates of the Incidence of 'Actual Innocence' Conviction," in 25 JUSTICE QUARTERLY [1], March, 2008. The study recognized the existence, not only of the Innocence Project (which has some spin-off projects in various law schools), but also of the Center on Wrongful Convictions at Northwestern University School of Law, and the Death Penalty Information Center. It further recognizes that some subjective evaluations have been made in reaching a conclusion that a wrongful conviction has occurred, but nevertheless suggests that the overall wrongful conviction estimate of ½ percent "extrapolates to about 5000 wrongful felony convictions and the imprisonment of more than 2,000 innocent persons in the United States every year."

While most wrongful convictions occurred because of an over reliance on erroneous eyewitness identifications, on poor defense lawyering, on wrongful failures of the prosecution to disclose evidence that cast a doubt on prosecution evidence, or on use of "snitch" testimony, there are also an unknown percentage of cases in which forensic evidence that was either unreliable or simply mistaken was used.

When criminal cases experience the utilization by incompetent, fraudulent, or deceptive experts on either side, not only is the issue inevitably raised of reversible error, but such instances also expose of problem of the ethics of forensic scientists—a topic explored in the next section of the text. As was noted elsewhere, in § 1.03, supra, the problem is real and it exists.[54]

VII. MISCELLANEOUS

§ 1.27 Bibliography of Additional References

Page 107, in "Bibliography," *insert the following entries alphabetically*:

Articles or books cited in footnotes are not necessarily repeated here

J. Vincent Aprille II, "Know the Ethics of the Expert Witness," CRIMINAL JUSTICE, Summer, 2006 at p. 45.

Diana Botluk & Elizabeth Fitterman, "Forensic Resources on the Web," in WILEY ENCYCLOPEDIA OF FORENSIC SCIENCE, 2009 [5] 2619.

Daniel A. Bronstein, *Law for the Expert Witness*, 3rd ed., 2007.

Kenneth S. Cohen, *Expert Witnessing and Scientific Testimony—Surviving in the Courtroom*, 2007.

Perry Hookman, *Medical Malpractice Expert Witnessing*, 2007.

Paul G. Giannelli, "Admissibility of Lab Reports: The Right of Confrontation Post-*Crawford*," CRIMINAL JUSTICE, Fall 2004, p. 26.

Paul C. Giannelli, "Prosecutors, Ethics, and Expert Witnesses," 76 FORDHAM L.REV. 1494 (2007).

Jason Krause, "E–Discovery Gets Real," ABA J., Feb. 2007, p. 44.

---

54. See also § 1.26, on Expert Witness Malpractice, infra.

Cross-examination, impeachment, ethical obligations, and malpractice actions based on expert conduct, are all inter-related issues that are taxing of the trial lawyer's ingenuity, perseverance, and skill. See also § 1.27 for additional bibliographical entries on the subjects.

Eleanor B. Kellett, Ed., "Discovery—All Things Electronic," (special issue) 3 THE SCITECHLAWYER, special issue of the Section of Science and Technology Law of the American Bar Association, Fall, 2007.

Jon May, "Experts and Notice: The When, The What, And The Why," 15 CRIM. JUST. SECT. NEWSL. (Issue 3) p. 7.

Andre A. Moenssens, "Ethics: Codes of Conduct for Expert Witnesses," article in WILEY ENCYCLOPEDIA OF FORENSIC SCIENCE (Jamieson, A. & Moenssens, A.A., eds.) 2009 [2] 957.

Sara Parikh & Terrence Lavin, "Lessons from Jury Research," 96 ILL. BAR J. 190 (2008).

Myrna S. Raeder, "See no Evil: Wrongful Convictions and the Prosecutorial Ethics of Offering Testimony by Jailhouse Informants and Dishonest Experts," 76 FORDHAM L.REV. 1413 (2007).

Jeffrey Toobin, "The CSI Effect," THE NEW YORKER, May 2007, p. 30.

Steven A. Saltzburg, "Changes to Model Rules Impact Prosecutors," CRIMINAL JUSTICE, Spring 2008, p. 1.

Joseph Sanders, "Expert Witness Ethics," 76 FORDHAM L.REV. 1539 (2007).

William C. Thompson, "Interpretation: Observer Effects," in WILEY ENCYCLOPEDIA OF FORENSIC SCIENCE, (Jamieson, A. & Moenssens, A.A., eds.) 2009 [3] 1575.

Don Wyckoff, "The Increasing Importance of Professional Certification and Accreditation," EVID. TECHNOL. MAG., March–April, 2008, p. 22.

Chapter 2

DEMONSTRATIVE EVIDENCE

I. INTRODUCTION

§ 2.01 Scope of the Chapter

Page 113. *Add to footnote 5:*

State v. Espiritu, 117 Hawai'i 127, 176 P.3d 885 (2008) (similarity doctrine); Roy v. St. Lukes Medical Center, 305 Wis.2d 658, 741 N.W.2d 256 (App.2007).

II. CASTS, MODELS, MAPS AND DRAWINGS

§ 2.02 Use of Casts and Models As Evidence

Page 114. *Add to footnote 1:*

Cloyd v. State, 943 So.2d 149 (Fla.App. 3 Dist. 2006) (14 beer mugs admitted to show quantity of alcohol consumed in intoxication case).

Page 114. *Add to footnote 3:*

State v. Reid, 213 S.W.3d 792 (Tenn.2006) (admission of styrofoam heads to aid medical examiner in locating victim's wounds proper).

Page 115. *Add to footnote 8:*

State v. Freeman, 269 S.W.3d 422 (Mo. 2008) (two Galliano liquor bottles admitted to show defendant possessed bottles on night of sexual assault and murder in light of unique shape of bottles); State v. Harrison, 213 S.W.3d 58 (Mo.App.2006) (use of button-up shirt to show what defendant wearing night of murder to show circumstances around murder and how victim's blood got on his shirt); Barry v. Quality Steel Products, 280 Conn. 1, 905 A.2d 55 (2006) (model of roof admitted in product liability suit to show conditions on day of the accident).

§ 2.03 Maps, Diagrams and Sketches

Page 117. *Add to footnote 1:*

Myers v. State, 887 N.E.2d 170 (Ind.App. 2008) (map admissible to show route taken by defendant and girlfriend to establish geographical knowledge of murder site); State v. Smith, 185 S.W.3d 747 (Mo.App.S.D. 2006) (diagram could be viewed by jury during deliberations after properly admitted to show orientation of the crime scene).

23

Page 118. *Add to footnote 2*:

United States v. Honken, 541 F.3d 1146 (8th Cir.2008) (maps admitted as statement against penal interest as intended use by recipient was to implicate other people in murders).

Page 118. *Add to footnote 4*:

But see, People v. Lewis, 43 Cal.4th 415, 75 Cal.Rptr.3d 588, 181 P.3d 947 (2008) (three cardboard drawings found in defendant's apartment rule inadmissible as hearsay because no evidence defendant made drawings).

III. PHOTOGRAPHIC EVIDENCE

§ 2.10 Motion Pictures and Videotape

Page 139. *Add to footnote 2*:

Commonwealth v. Geiger, 944 A.2d 85 (Pa.Super.2008).

Page 139. *Add to footnote 5*:

Page v. State, 934 A.2d 891 (Del.Super.2007) (crime scene video of close-ups of victim and blood on the ground relevant to aid in jury understanding of expert testimony and to show killing intentional. Gruesomeness of images does not make video per se inadmissible); Brooks v. State, 973 So.2d 380 (Ala.Crim.App.2007) (video of crime scene taken from police patrol car admissible to show remoteness of crime scene and defendant's efforts to conceal his crime); United States v. Perez–Gonzalez, 445 F.3d 39 (1st Cir.2006) (video taken by news photographers of the crime as it occurred relevant to support testimony of witnesses).

IV. PHOTOGRAPHIC EVIDENCE IN GENERAL

§ 2.13 Admissibility of Photographs

1. IN GENERAL

Page 151. *Add to footnote 7*:

Bevel v. State, 983 So.2d 505 (Fla.2008) (photographs of victim's bedroom, including bloodstained mattress, admissible to show perspective of the shooter); Banta v. State, 282 Ga. 392, 651 S.E.2d 21 (2007) (photos taken by emergency responders of defendant's clutter-filled apartment probative as to the obstacles the responders encountered upon arrival, disputed defendant's version of how victim was injured and his efforts to aid victim); State v. Wakefield, 190 N.J. 397, 921 A.2d 954 (2007) (photo of debris covered area with indistinct bodies probative and relevant to corroborate existence of aggravating or mitigating factors); Shuffield v. State, 189 S.W.3d 782 (Tex.Crim.App. 2006) (photos depicting view of room where crime occurred and fully clothed victim probative to support the testimony about the condition of the crime scene).

Page 151. *Add to footnote 8:*

Chamberlin v. State, 989 So.2d 320 (Miss. 2008) (photos of two bodies in freezers and wrapped in blankets, as they appeared at crime scene, admissible to show circumstances of death, location of the bodies and cause of death); People v. Watson, 43 Cal.4th 652, 76 Cal.Rptr.3d 208, 182 P.3d 543 (2008) (crime scene photos of victim's body, in its entirety and in parts, from different angles and blood spatter surrounding body admissible to illustrate motive and intent to kill); People v. Hoyos, 41 Cal.4th 872, 63 Cal.Rptr.3d 1, 162 P.3d 528 (2007); Dampier v. State, 973 So.2d 221 (Miss.2008) (photos depicting bloody crime scene and blood spatter probative as to the circumstances of the murder); Sanders v. State, 939 So.2d 842 (Miss.App.2006) (photos of arrangement of victims' bodies and wounds taken at crime scene relevant to show circumstances of death and cause of death).

Page 152. *Add to footnote 9:*

People v. Rhodes, 49 A.D.3d 668, 853 N.Y.S.2d 375 (N.Y.A.D.2 Dept.2008) (black and white photographs of victim and victim's wounds relevant to support elements of second-degree murder, criminal possession of weapon and corroborated witness testimony); State v. Ware, 980 So.2d 730 (La.App. 3 Cir.2008) (photos depicting images of victim's corpse and wounds suffered relevant to show nature of the injuries in light of defendant's claim of self-defense); State v. Rios, 234 S.W.3d 412 (Mo.App.W.D. 2007) (photos of victim's wounds, blood soaked ground and insects on wounds probative as to the scene of the crime, nature of the wounds, and the condition of the body upon discovery); People v. Alvarez, 38 A.D.3d 930, 830 N.Y.S.2d 848 (N.Y.A.D. 3 Dept.2007) (close-up photo of victim's neck injury aided medical examiner in showing the nature of the wound, the intent to murder and the type of weapon used. Photographs of the victim's body were relevant to refute defendant's claim that he moved the body after finding the victim dead); Davis v. State, 368 Ark. 401, 246 S.W.3d 862 (2007); White v. State, 964 So.2d 1181 (Miss.App.2007) (admission of photos depicting victim's mangled body proper to show circumstances of death, cause of death and location of the body); State v. Blank, 955 So.2d 90 (La.2007); Davis v. State, 368 Ark. 401, 246 S.W.3d 862 (2007) (poster-size photos of victim at the crime scene probative to refute defendant's claim of self-defense as they showed intent to kill and placement of wounds); State v. Watson, 227 S.W.3d 622 (Tenn.Crim.App.2006) (photos of crime scene from a distance and close-up pictures of blood spatter on victim's chest relevant to show location of the body and close-range of the fatal gunshots).

Page 152. *Add to footnote 10:*

State v. Crum, 286 Kan. 145, 184 P.3d 222 (2008); Browning v. State, 134 P.3d 816 (Okla.Crim.App.2006).

Page 153. *Add to footnote 16:*

State v. Diar, 120 Ohio St.3d 460, 900 N.E.2d 565 (2008) (photographs of the victim's charred body at the crime scene and in the coroner's office, including an images of charred and exposed brain tissue and bodily fluids, admissible to explain medical examiner's testimony and establish an intent to kill); Mack v. State, 188 P.3d 1284 (Okla.Crim.App.2008) (photographs of victims' incinerated bodies should not have been admitted as the they did not die from burns and the images tended to inflame the jury. However, the error was harmless).

Page 154. *Add to footnote 18:*

England v. State, 940 So.2d 389 (Fla.2006).

Page 154. *Add to footnote 20:*

Ratliff v. Commonwealth, 194 S.W.3d 258 (Ky.2006); Dant v. Commonwealth, 258 S.W.3d 12 (Ky.2008); Broadhead v. State, 981 So.2d 320 (Miss.App.2007); Banks v. State, 281 Ga. 678, 642 S.E.2d 679 (2007); Casey v. State, 215 S.W.3d 870 (Tex.Crim. App.2007).

Page 154. *Add to footnote 21:*

Tejera v. McCollum, 2008 WL 5102881 (S.D.Fla.2008) (admission of three nude photos of victim lying in the street proper to show condition of body when it was found, efforts to revive the victim and attempts to locate the killer's fingerprints on the body); Williams v. State, 188 P.3d 208 (Okla.Crim.App.2008) (nude photo of victim at medical examiner's office, including images of surgical sutures, relevant to show nature and extent of inflicted wounds).

Page 155. *Add to footnote 23:*

People v. Ortiz, 155 P.3d 532 (Colo.App. 2006).

Page 156. *Add to footnote 26:*

Banks v. State, 281 Ga. 678, 642 S.E.2d 679 (2007) (post-incision autopsy photos needed to show injury to under the scalp and to the brain not otherwise visible).

Compare, Overton v. State, 295 Ga. App. 223, 671 S.E.2d 507 (2008) (introduction of pre-and post-autopsy photos of the victims in a RICO trial error. The pictures showed an exposed brain, skin pulled back from the scalp to reveal a gunshot wound and a wooden dowel inserted into the skull. Photos did not illustrate a material given the defendants were not charged with murder, did not assert a claim of self-defense, and were will to stipulate to the killings. However, the error found the error to harmless in light of other evidence.)

Page 156. *Add to footnote 30:*

People v. Villalobos, 159 P.3d 624 (Colo. App.2006); State v. Holmes, 758 N.W.2d 326 (Minn.App.2008).

3. COLOR PHOTOGRAPHS

Page 158. *Add to footnote 35:*

Whitmire v. State, 183 S.W.3d 522 (Tex. App.—Houston 2006) (close-up of gunshot wound to the head admissible as it helped the jury to understand the nature of the injuries and cause of death. Further, the image was not enlarged or altered and is not even referenced in the testimony.); Randall v. State, 232 S.W.3d 285 (Tex. App.—Beaumont 2007) (crime scene photos of victim inflicted with 90 stab wounds at dump site and during autopsy admissible to show nature of wounds. The gruesome nature of the injuries created by the actions of the defendants does not render the images inadmissible.)

Page 158. *Add to footnote 36:*

Llamas v. State, 270 S.W.3d 274 (Tex. App.—Amarillo 2008).

Page 158. *Add to footnote 37:*

People v. Howard, 42 Cal.4th 1000, 71 Cal. Rptr.3d 264, 175 P.3d 13 (2008); State v. Johnson, 244 S.W.3d 144 (Mo.2008).

4. SLIDES

Page 160. *Add to footnote 45*:

Sneed v. State, 1 So.3d 104 (Ala.Crim.App. 2007) (slides of victim injuries admissible to support medical examiner's testimony).

§ 2.14   Gruesome and Inflammatory Photographs

Page 162. *Add to footnote 2*:

Middleton v. Roper, 498 F.3d 812 (8th Cir. 2007) (photos of victims' skeletonized bodies admissible to illustrate expert medical testimony and to corroborate testimony on defendant's prior crimes for sentencing purposes); Mitchell v. State, 136 P.3d 671 (Okla.Crim.App.2006) (death sentence reversed and remanded for reconsideration when sentencing jury received many more gruesome images of the victims at the crime scene and during the autopsy than the jury during the original trial. The additional photographs were unnecessarily cumulative and inflammatory); State v. Warledo, 286 Kan. 927, 190 P.3d 937 (2008) (photo of victim at crime scene showing beaten, bloody, and partially charred body and autopsy photograph of victim's face with visible shoe mark admissible to establish layout of the crime scene and violence used to perpetrate the killing).

Page 163. *Add to footnote 7*:

State v. Hill, 250 S.W.3d 855 (Mo.App.2008) (photo of autopsy of child depicting subdural hematoma admissible to show extent and nature of injuries in Shaken Baby Syndrome case when defendant repeatedly challenged the medical evidence of the cause of death).

Page 163. *Add to footnote 8*:

Smith v. State, 984 So.2d 295 (Miss.App. 2007) (pictures of victim in pool of blood and during the autopsy establish time interval of death and identity of the victim); State v. Young, 196 S.W.3d 85 (Tenn.2006) (photo of victim facedown in morgue with stab would visible admissible to supplement medical testimony on the cause of death).

§ 2.15   Identification Photographs

1.   "MUG SHOTS"

Page 166. *Add to footnote 2*:

State v. Smith, 110 Conn.App. 70, 954 A.2d 202 (2008).

Page 166. *Add to footnote 5*:

United States v. Condrin, 473 F.3d 1283 (10th Cir.2007) (photo of defendant taken by border patrol agent necessary to explain testimony defendant was bald but appeared in courtroom with full head of hair and beard.)

Page 166. *Add to footnote 7*:

State v. Collins, 100 Conn.App. 833, 919 A.2d 1087 (2007) (while the mug shot of the defendant should not have been admitted when defendant stipulated to his involvement in the events in question, its admission was not prejudicial because it did not contain markings to indicate it was a police photograph).

§ 2.16   Evidence Resulting From Special Photographic Techniques

Page 173. *Add to footnote 8*:

See also, Renzi v. Paredes, 452 Mass. 38, 890 N.E.2d 806 (2008) (digital images of mammography film admissible to help jury understand the original mammogram x-rays).

———

V. MOTION PICTURES AND VIDEOTAPE IN COURT

§ 2.17   Admissibility of Motion Pictures as Evidence

Page 174. *Add to footnote 2*:

Jones v. DHR Cambridge Homes, Inc., 381 Ill.App.3d 18, 319 Ill.Dec. 59, 885 N.E.2d 330 (1 Dist.2008).

§ 2.18   Admissibility of Videotapes in Court

Page 176. *Add to footnote 2*:

People v. Armijo, 179 P.3d 134 (Colo.App. 2007)—surveillance video.

Page 177. *Add to footnote 3*:

But see, Washington v. State, 406 Md. 642, 961 A.2d 1110 (2008) (surveillance video and photos were inadmissible because the state failed to lay a proper foundation when it did not produced testimony on how the images were created, stored, and transferred to a videotape).

Page 177. *Add to footnote 5*:

Gissendanner v. State, 949 So.2d 956 (Ala. Crim.App.2006); Epperson v. Commonwealth, 197 S.W.3d 46 (Ky.2006); Floyd v. State, 2008 WL 3989540 (Ala.Crim.App. Aug. 29, 2008).

Page 177. *Add to footnote 8*:

Shennett v. State, 937 So.2d 287 (Fla.App. 4 Dist.2006) (video reenactment created by investigating officer, depicting defendant breaking a van window using pieces of porcelain during a burglary, was not admissible because the experiment was not conducted under similar conditions. The defendant threw the porcelain from a crouched position to break the window and the police officer stood up to throw the projectile and the window did not shatter.)

Page 178. *Add to footnote 9*:

Watson v. State, 2008 WL 4981263 (Miss. App.2008).

Page 178. *Add to footnote 10*:

People v. McCree, 366 Ill.App.3d 290, 304 Ill.Dec. 9, 852 N.E.2d 259 (1 Dist.2006) (video of defendant statement admissible as a party admission and to impeach his testimony when he changed his story about why he killed the victim in two statements and while testifying at trial).

Page 178. *Add to footnote 11*:

Lemus v. State, 162 P.3d 497 (Wyo.2007); People v. Campbell, 33 A.D.3d 716, 826 N.Y.S.2d 267 (N.Y.A.D. 2 Dept.2006); Jackson v. State, 163 P.3d 596 (Okla.Crim.App. 2007) (court was not legally required to review 20–hour interrogation in its entirety before admitting at trial when defendant failed to object to specific portions of the recording. Further, the video interrogation was relevant to elucidate the multiple versions of the killing offered by defendant, and he claimed the defense of voluntary intoxication.)

But see, State v. Gonzalez, 282 Kan. 73, 145 P.3d 18 (2006) (admission of video of unredacted police interview abuse of discretion when it contained statements about other crimes and evidence was irrelevant as to motive, opportunity, intent, preparation, plan, and knowledge. However, error was harmless as the defendant offered his own confession to the crime and the video was introduced by the interviewing officer who was available to clarify the content.)

VI. COMPUTER ANIMATION AND SIMULATION

§ 2.19 Computer Technology as a Visual Aid

Page 179. *Add to footnote 2*:

Howell v. Union Pacific R. Co., 980 So.2d 854 (La.App. 3 Cir.2008) (expert-created animation depicting a train accident was admissible to illustrate expert's opinion); Roy v. St. Lukes Medical Center, 305 Wis.2d 658, 741 N.W.2d 256 (App.2007) (animations depicting how stent became dislodged in a medical malpractice case admissible as the expert admitted the animation was an approximation what he thought happened and it was only used to support the expert's theory of plaintiff's case); Hudson v. City of Chicago, 378 Ill.App.3d 373, 317 Ill.Dec. 262, 881 N.E.2d 430 (1 Dist.2007) (computer simulation of collusion was admissible to show willful and wanton conduct by a police officer when it was based on data from the record and supported by witness testimony).

Page 179. *Add to footnote 3*:

Commonwealth v. Hardy, 918 A.2d 766 (Pa.Super.2007) (short computer animation explaining Shaken Baby Syndrome admissible to support medical testimony).

But see, People v. Unger, 278 Mich. App. 210, 749 N.W.2d 272 (2008) (computer animation depicting possible explanation of victim's injuries in a murder case based on medical considerations was not admissible when the expert was a biomechanical engineer and not a doctor. Further, the information used to form the basis of the conjectured chain of events was inconsistent with the facts in evidence and thus irrelevant to the issues of the case.)

VII.   MISCELLANEOUS

§ 2.20   Selected Sources, Bibliography, and Additional References

Page 186. *Add to Articles*:

Mark Cammarck, "Admissibility of Evidence to Prove Undisputed Facts: A Comparison of the California Evidence Code § 210 and Federal Rule of Evidence 401," 36 Sw. U. L. Rev. 879 (2008).

Douglas Page, "Forensics Focuses on Digital Photography," 1 Forensics Mag. 10 (Summer, 2006).

Chapter 3

CHEMICAL AND OTHER TESTS FOR ALCOHOLIC INTOXICATION

————

I. ALCOHOL INTOXICATION TESTING

§ 3.07 Passive Alcohol Screening Devices

Page 214, at the end of § 3.07, *insert the following text*:

There are other relatively inexpensive personal breath alcohol screeners on the market. Among them are two instruments recently released by Alcohawk®. Each personal BAC screener is reported to contain state-of-the-art oxide sensors to accurately estimate the breath alcohol content in seconds. It requires blowing into a mouthpiece that is a part of the hand-held instrument. The BAC reading appears on a small LCD to the nearest 0.01% in the key chain Micro instrument. The other instrument measures BAC op to o.40% in an FDA-cleared ABI model. It is touted as the only DOT/NHTSA approved personal BAC breath screener on the market, and obtains about 300 tests on a 9–volt battery. The unit is marketed with a dashboard socket adapter as well, and reportedly is advertised for $99.95 for the "professional grade" instrument. As of early 2009, we are not aware of any validity testing in connection with either of the two screening instruments.

§ 3.08 Standards of Intoxication

Page 214. *Insert the following corrections in footnote 2*:

The cited U.S. Code Annotated (USCA) sections are no longer current. The new corresponding sections are stated here:

Sec. 2707(f)(4) is to be replaced by Sec. 31310(a);

Sec. 2708(a)(3) is to be replaced by Sec. 31311(a)(3);

Sec. 2710(a) is to be replaced by Sec. 31314(a).

Page 215. *Add the following to footnote 3*:

More recently developed breath-alcohol testing instruments are today available. See, e.g., discussions on the Intoxilyzer 8000, the Draegers 7110 and 7419, the In-toximeter EC/IR, and the Data Master, in Lawrence Taylor & Steven Oberman, *Drunk Driving Defense*, 6th Edition (2008).

————

II. EVIDENCE OF ALCOHOL INTOXICATION

§ 3.12 Legal Aspects of Chemical Tests

3. EVIDENCE OF REFUSAL TO SUBMIT TO CHEMICAL TEST

Page 234. *Add the following text to footnote 20*:

The Supreme Court of Utah reversed the Court of Appeals decision in 2007. See, State v. Rodriguez, 156 P.3d 771 (2007), holding that the per se exigent circumstances status does not apply to seizures of blood for gathering blood-alcohol evidence, and that under the totality of circumstances analysis, probable cause as well as exigent circumstances justified the warrantless drawing of blood from the defendant.

III. MISCELLANEOUS

§ 3.17 Bibliography of Additional References

Beginning on Page 241, *insert in appropriate alphabetical order the following*:

Eugene R. Bertolli, Constantine J. Forkiotis, R. Robert Pannone & Hazel Dawkins, "A Behavioral Optometry/Vision Science Perspective on the Horizontal Gaze Nystagmus Exam for DUI Enforcement," THE FORENSIC EXAMINER, Spring 2007, p. 26.

Chancey C. Fessler, Frederich A. Tulleners, David G. Howitt & John R. Richards, "Determination of mouth alcohol using the Draeger Evidential Portable Alcohol System," 48 SCIENCE AND JUSTICE 16 (2007).

Patrick N. Friel, Barry K. Logan & John Baer, "An Evaluation of the Reliability of Widmark Calculations Based on Breath Alcohol Measurements," 40 J. FORENSIC SCI. 91 (1994).

R. G. Gullberg, "Employing components-of-variance to evaluate forensic breath test instruments," 48 SCIENCE AND JUSTICE 2 (2008).

Helen Gunnarson, "New DUI Bill replaces JDPs [judicial driving permits] with 'monitoring device driving permits,' " 95 ILL. BAR J. 398 (2007).

Allan Wayne Jones & Lars Anderson, "Variability of the Blood/Breath Alcohol Ratio in Drinking Drivers," 41 J. FORENSIC SCI. 916 (1996).

Allan Wayne Jones, "Alcohol–Methods of Analysis in Body Fluids and Breath," WILEY ENCYCLOPEDIA OF FORENSIC SCIENCE, 2009.

A. R. Stowell & L. I. Stowell, "Estimation of Blood Alcohol Concentrations after Social Drinking," 43 J. FORENSIC SCI. 14 (1998).

Page 243, in the entry of Lawrence Taylor's treatise, *replace the entry with the following updated entry*:

Lawrence Taylor & Steven Oberman, *Drunk Driving Defense* (6th Edition with Forms on CD), 2008–Aspen Publishers.

Chapter 4

SCIENTIFIC DETECTION OF SPEEDING

————

II. RADAR SPEED DETECTION

§ 4.02 Principles of Radar Speed Detection

Page 248, *footnote 5, replace the existing reference with the following*:

http://www.mphindustries.com.

§ 4.03 Factors Affecting Reliability

Page 254, *replace the existing references in footnote 1 with the following*:

http://www.theiacp.org/profassist/IACPATR RadarModule6104R1.pdf; http://www.the iacp.org/profassist/IACPDTRRadarModule 6104R1.pdf;

§ 4.04 Required Testing of Equipment

Page 254, *replace the asterisk footnote by the more recent source*:

http://www.nhtsa.dot.gov/portal/nhtsa static file downloader.jsp?file=/static files/DOT/ NHTSA/TrafficInjuryControl/Articles/Asso ciatedFiles/810845.pdf In addition to the tests mentioned above, the 2007 edition also lists "signal processing" as one of the tests.

————

V. EVIDENCE OF SPEEDING

§ 4.10 Admissibility of Radar Speed Readings

Page 266, at the end of footnote 11, *insert*:

West's Fla.Stat.Ann. Title 13 Sec. 316.1906(2) (2008).

§ 4.14 Evidence of LASER ("LIDAR") and Photo Radar Speed Detection

Page 272, at the end of footnote 4, *add the following*:

See also, City of Upper Arlington v. Limbert, 138 Ohio Misc.2d 30, 856 N.E.2d 336 (2006): laser speed detector, used by law enforcement officers to detect when motorists are speeding, is a reliable and accurate scientific measure of the speed of a moving object, if the device is used in accordance with certain procedures delineated by the manufacturer. Among these procedures are that the laser is pointed so that the red dot on the scope is aligned with the reflective area on the target vehicle; the target is moving either directly toward or away from the laser at no more than a slight angle; and the laser was properly calibrated prior to use. The calibration consists of the self-test operated within the instrument itself, and a measurement at a distance on a test range where the distance test is conducted on the test range before use of the instrument at each shift, with a laser measuring a known distance.

Page 273, at the end of the text in § 4.14, *insert the following new footnote 9:*

9. An unsigned bulletin circulated on the Internet, sent from an "allegedly reliable source" to a group of attorneys, announced that the State of Illinois would begin to use photo-radar in July of 2007 in highway work zones on Interstates where speeds are lowered to 45 mph, Violators will receive a $375 ticket in the mail for a first offense and $1,000 for a second offense, for which also a 90–day driver's license would be imposed. This penalty structure is reportedly the harshest yet for a city or state using photo speed enforcement. Since drivers also would be reported to suffer demerit points against their driving permits, insurance companies would be allowed tgo raise their rates for drivers proven to have violated the speeding laws. Two camera vans were scheduled to be used, issuing tickets after the taking of photographs of both the driver's face and the license plate. See also, http://www.dot.state.ill.us/press/r033005.html.

VI.   MISCELLANEOUS

§ 4.15   Bibliography of Additional References

Page 275, in the reference for National Conference of State Legislatures, *insert the following updated reference to:*

http://www.ncsl.org/programs/transportation/radar.htm.

Chapter 5

FORENSIC ACCOUNTING

VI. MISCELLANEOUS

§ 5.10 Bibliography of Selected References

Beginning on Page 308, *insert the following additional sources*:

S. Gregory Boyd & Matthew E. Moersfelder, "Global Business in the Metaverse—Money Laundering and Securities Fraud," THE SCITECH LAWYER, Winter 2007, p. 4.

Jan Colbert, "What the 10 New Accounting Standards Mean for Forensic Accountants," THE FORENSIC EXAMINER, Winter 2007, p. 32.

Anna Lysyanskaya, "How to Keep Secrets Safe," SCIENTIFIC AMERICAN, Sept. 2008, p. 89.

George A. Manning, *Financial Investigation and Forensic Accounting*, CRC Press 2005.

Zabihollah Rezace, "The Role of Forensic Auditing Techniques in Restoring Public Trust and Investor Confidence in Financial Information," THE FORENSIC EXAMINER, Spring 2007, p. 44.

Chapter 6

FORENSIC COMPUTER ANALYSIS

III. TRIAL AIDS

§ 6.10 Identifying Experts and Training

4. EXPERT REFERRALS

Page 344, at the end of "4. Expert Referrals," *insert the following paragraph*:

On February 20, 2008, the American Academy of Forensic Sciences, a leading international membership association to which in excess of 5,000 forensic scientists belong, created a new section within the Academy called the Digital & Multimedia Sciences section. It had been 28 years since the Academy last created a new section when it embraced a Forensic Engineering section. While the members of this section may have interests that are broader than merely computer forensics, many leading experts are among the new section's members.

IV. MISCELLANEOUS

§ 6.13 Bibliography of Additional References and Sources of Further Study

Beginning on Page 353, *insert in the appropriate locations the following*:

Richard Acellom "Feds Ready to Tackle Cybercrime," ABA J., Feb. 2009, p. 37.

John J. Barbara, "Quality Assurance Practices for Computer Forensics—Part 2," FORENSIC MAGAZINE, April–May, 2007, p. 54.

John J. Barbara, "Quality Assurance Practices for Computer Forensics—Part 2," FORENSIC MAGAZINE, June–July, 2007, p. 54.

John J. Barbara, "Documenting Computer Forensic Procedures," FORENSIC MAGAZINE, Oct.-Nov. 2007, p. 56.

John J. Barbara, "Computer Forensics Standards and Controls," FORENSIC MAGAZINE, Dec. 2007, p. 10.

Whitfield Diffie & Susan Landau, "Brave New World of Wiretapping," SCIENTIFIC AMERICAN, Sep. 2008, p. 57.

Thomas A. Johnson, *Forensic Computer Crime Investigation,* CRC PRESS, 2006.

William J. Haddad, Hon., "Authentication and Identification of E–Mail Evidence," 96 ILL. BAR J. 252 (2008).

Anna Lysyanskaya, "How to Keep Secrets Safe," SCIENTIFIC AMERICAN, Sep. 2008, p. 89.

Keven Mandia & Kris Harms, "Don't Forget Your Memory," FORENSIC MAGAZINE, Dec. 2007–Jan. 2009, p. 22.

Gavin W. Manes, "Digital Forensics in the Twenty-first Century," THE FORENSIC EXAMINER, Winter, 2007, p. 12.

Meredith Mullins, "Electronic Heath Records—A Double–Edged Scalpel," THE SCITECH LAWYER, Winter, 2009, p. 4.

David Navetta, "The Legal Implications, Risks, and Problems of the PCI Data Security Standard," THE SCITECH LAWYER, Summer, 2008, p. 4.

Ira P. Rothken, "Moredata–Electronic Discovery and Evidence," at http://Fwww.Fmoredata.com/?gclid=CLS01dXYyIsCFQkGQQodVRi Dw.

Dan Swanson, "Auditing Information Security: Are You Protected?" THE SCITECH LAWYER, Summer, 2008, p. 16.

K. Van Waalrijk van Doren, M. Den Dunnen & Zeno Geradts, "Computers," in WILEY ENCYCLOPEDIA OF FORENSIC SCIENCE, 2009 [2] 584.

*

EVIDENCE BASED ON THE

Part IIPhysical Sciences

Chapter 7

FORENSIC DOCUMENT EXAMINATION

————

II. THE EXAMINATION OF FORENSIC–RELATED DOCUMENTS

§ 7.04 Standards of Comparison

1. HANDWRITING

Page 365, at the end of footnote 2, *add the following text:*

A similar comprehensive treatment of forensic document examination topics is spread through the new Wiley Encyclopedia of Forensic Science. In its 5 volumes, published in 2009, can be found a number of articles on document examination, by prominent authorities in the field who offer a world-wide perspective on their topics. The print version of this reference work is due to be updated annually online, which updates will be made available by subscription. A few of the significant contributions to the literature and science relative to document examinations to be found in the Encyclopedia are listed herein in this Supplement, infra, in § 7.23.

§ 7.11 The Comparison of Printed Matter

Page 389, at the end of footnote 1, *add the following text:*

See also, David Mazella Williams, "Micro–Raman Spectroscopy of Color Inkjet Printed Documents," 9 J.AMERICAN SOC. OF QUESTIONED DOCUMENT EXAMINERS [1] 1 (2006).

————

III. EVIDENCE OF FORENSIC DOCUMENT EXAMINATIONS

§ 7.17 Evidence of Handwriting Comparisons

Page 404, at the end of the section, *add the new subsection*:

5. THE NATIONAL ACADEMY OF SCIENCES 2009 REPORT

As was already well known among forensic scientists at the time this Supplement became available, the National Academy of Science, on February 18, 2009, released its Report on Strengthening Forensic Science in the United States. The Report's main provisions, which were analyzed in some detail in the Chapter 1 of this Supplement,[1] was critical of a number of forensic science disciplines, and made a few brief comments about forensic document examination as well. This was, of course, no surprise to any document examiner since the sub-specialty of handwriting comparisons of their discipline was the first to suffer the brunt of attorney attacks on *Daubert* grounds, as is described in the main text on beginning at page 401.

Considering the broad criticism leveled against many impression comparison techniques in the NAS Report, its treatment of handwriting comparisons technique was relatively mild. Perhaps that was because, since the early challenges to handwriting comparisons, considerable research in handwriting methodology and in the ability of trained examiners to differentiate between intra-writer and inter-writer characteristics. Today, a greater understanding exists about the individuality and persistence of handwriting characteristics. Or perhaps it was because, unlike the firearm-toolmark and fingerprint disciplines, the handwriting. examiners make no claims of all-or-nothing conclusions,[2] but instead express opinions on a graded scale of nine possible levels of the examiner's confidence in a conclusion reach, as is described in the main text in § 7.06, on page 375.

All that the Report stated was that "The scientific basis for handwriting comparisons needs to be strengthened."[3] It further recognized that in light of intensive research conducted in the last decade or more, "there may be" a scientific basis for handwriting comparisons, "at least in the absence of intentional obfuscation or forgery."[4]

The NAS Report also discussed briefly ink analyses discussed in § 7.12 of the main text (on page 389), but refrained from commenting on its view of the validity of findings based on ink analysis because it had not received sufficient input on that topic.

---

1. Supra p. 4 of this Supplement.

2. The NAS Report was scornful fingerprint examiners who testified to a zero percent error rate, or to positive matches, as do some firearm and toolmark examiners. See, in this regard, this Supplement at Chapter 1, supra, and at Chapters 8 and 10, infra.

3. NAS Report, page 5–30.

4. Id.

V. MISCELLANEOUS

§ 7.23 Bibliography of Selected References

Page 414, *insert the following additional sources*:

Valery N. Aginsky, "Using TLC and GC–MS to Determine Whether Inks Came from the same Manufacturing Batch," J. AM.SOC. OF QUESTIONED DOCUMENT EXAMINERS, Vol. 9 [1] 19 (2006).

Chris Anderson, "Limited Populations—Are They Feasible for Handwriting Examinations?" J. AM.SOC. OF QUESTIONED DOCUMENT EXAMINERS, Vol. 9 [1] 19 (2006).

Danna E. Bicknell & Gerald M. LaPorte, "Forged and Counterfeit Documents," in WILEY ENCYCLOPEDIA OF FORENSIC SCIENCE (Jamieson, A. & Moenssens, A.A., eds.) 2009 [3] 1255.

Antonio A. Cantu, "Ink Analysis," in WILEY ENCYCLOPEDIA OF FORENSIC SCIENCE (Jamieson, A. & Moenssens, A.A., eds.) 2009 [3] 1841.

Stephen P. Day, "Handwriting and Signatures," in WILEY ENCYCLOPEDIA OF FORENSIC SCIENCE (Jamieson, A. & Moenssens, A.A., eds.) 2009 [3] 1451.

Adrian G. Dyer, Bryan Found & Doug Rogers, "An Insight into Forensic Document Examiner Expertise for Discriminating Between Forged and Disguised Signatures," 53 J. FORENSIC SCI. 1154 (2008).

Celine Equey, Raymond Marquis & Williams D. Mazella, "Influence of Writing Posture on the Dimensions of Signatures," J. AM. SOC. OF QUESTIONED DOC. EXAMINERS, Vol. 10 [1] p. 53 (2007).

Bryan Found, "The Forensic Examination of Handwritten Text and Signatures," in WILEY Encyclopedia of Forensic Science (JAMIESON, A. & MOENSSENS, A.A., EDS.) 2009 [3] 1841.

Linda Hart & Lamar Miller, "Microsoft Access in the Questioned Document Laboratory," J. AM. SOC. OF QUESTIONED DOC. EXAMINERS, Vol. 10 [2] 71 (2007).

Brian Lindblom & Robert Gervais, "A Review of Write–On^2 Document Comparison Software (Part 1)," ABFDE NEWS, Jan. 2008, p. 7.

S. D. Maind, N. Chattapadhyay, Ch. Gandhi, S. C. Kumar & M. Sudersanan, "Quantitative evaluation of europium in blue ballpoint pen inks/offset printing inks tagged with europium thenoyltrifluoroacetonate," 48 SCIENCE & JUSTICE 61 (2008).

Williams D. Mazella, "Forensic Image Analysis of Laser–Printed Documents," AM. SOC. OF QUESTIONED DOCUMENT EXAMINERS, Vol. 9 [1] p. 19 (2007).

W. D. Mazzella, "Interpretation: Document Evidence," in WILEY ENCYCLOPEDIA OF FORENSIC SCIENCE (Jamieson, A. & Moenssens, A.A., eds.) 2009 [3] 1557.

John P. Murphy, "Paper Analysis," in WILEY ENCYCLOPEDIA OF FORENSIC SCIENCE (Jamieson, A. & Moenssens, A.A., eds.) 2009 [4] 1968.

Cedric Neumann, "Ink Comparison and Interpretations," in WILEY ENCYCLOPEDIA OF FORENSIC SCIENCE (Jamieson, A. & Moenssens, A.A., eds.) 2009 [3] 1546.

Raymond Orta M. & Magdalena Ezcurra G., "Neurosciences Applied to Handwriting Examination," J. AM. SOC. QUESTIONED DOCUMENT EXAMINERS, Vol. 10 [2] p. 63 (2007).

Kaitline Papson, Sylvia Stachura, Luka Boralsky & John Allison, "Identification of Colorants in Pigmented Pen Inks By Laser Desorption Mass Spectrometry," 53 J. FORENSIC SCIENCE 100 (2008).

Atul K. Singla, O. P asuja & Sarbjit Kaur, "The Effect of Water Soakings on Ballpoint Pen Inks," J. AM. SOC. QUESTIONED DOCUMENT EXAMINERS, Vol. 10 [2] p. 97 (2007).

Farrell C. Shiver, "Intersecting Lines," in WILEY ENCYCLOPEDIA OF FORENSIC SCIENCE (Jamieson, A. & Moenssens, A.A., eds.) 2009 [3] 1594.

Gordon A. I. Sharpe, "Intersecting Lines: Documents," WILEY ENCYCLOPEDIA OF FORENSIC SCIENCE (Jamieson, A. & Moenssens, A.A., eds.) 2009 [5] 2660.

Patrick Van Eecke, "Electronic Signatures in Europe," THE SCITECH LAWYER, Summer 2007, p. 10.

John Welch, "Erasable Ink; something old, something new," 48 SCIENCE AND JUSTICE 187 (2008).

Celine Weyermann, Beatrice Schiffer, & Pierre Margot, "A logical framework to ballpoint ink dating Interpretation," 48 SCIENCE AND JUSTICE 117 (2008).

Chapter 8

FIREARM AND TOOLMARK IDENTIFICATION

III. PRINCIPLES OF FIREARMS IDENTIFICATION

§ 8.08 Bullet Identification

Page 445, line 3, before the words "Figure 9," *insert the following text*:

Opinions with respect to the outcome of a comparison are expressed as falling in one of four categories. They are: (1) *Identification*— "where there is agreement of a combination of individual characteristics and all discernable class characteristics where the extent of agreement exceeds that which can occur in comparison of tool marks made by different tools and is consistent with the agreement demonstrated by toolmarks known to have been produced by the same tool"; (2) *Inconclusive*—where there is "some agreement of individual characteristics and all class characteristics, but insufficient for an identification"; or where there is agreement of all discernible class characteristics without agreement or disagreement of all individual characteristics due to an absence, insufficiency, or lack of reproducibility; or where there is "agreement of all discernible class characteristics and disagreement of individual characteristics, but insufficient for an elimination"; (3) *Elimination*—where there is "significant disagreement of discernible class characteristics and/or individual characteristics"; (4) *Unsuitable*—where the evidence is "unsuitable for comparison."[1]

In United States v. Glynn,[2] a *Daubert* challenge to bar the expert from expressing his opinion "to a reasonable degree of ballistic certainty" was successful. The firearms examiner tied a bullet retrieved from the victim's body and shell casing from two related crime scenes to a firearm linked to the defendant. The court, drawing on United States v. Monteiro,[3] concluded that "ballistics examination not only lacks the rigor of science but suffers from greater uncertainty than many other kinds of forensic evidence. Yet its methodology has garnered sufficient empirical support as to warrant its admissibility as evidence. . . . The problem is how to admit it into evidence without giving the jury the impression—always a risk where forensic evidence is concerned—that it

---

1. The quoted portions are from "AFTE Criteria for Identification Committee—Theory of Identification, Range of Striae Comparison Reports and Modified Glossary of Definitions," AFTE Journal, 1992:24(2):336–340.

2. 578 F.Supp.2d 567 (S.D.N.Y.2008).

3. 407 F.Supp.2d 351 (D.Mass.2006), cited at page 476 of the main text, at footnote 8.

has greater reliability than its imperfect methodology permits." To solve that quandary, the District Judge ruled that, on retrial, the expert's opinion would be permitted to be stated in terms of "more likely than not," but nothing more.

———

V. EVIDENCE OF FIREARM, AMMUNITION, AND TOOLMARK EXAMINATIONS

§ 8.18   Bullet-to-Firearm Matching

Page 474, at the end of the third paragraph, and before the start of the next section, *insert the following text*:

THE NATIONAL ACADEMY OF SCIENCES 2009 REPORT

The National Academy of Science, on February 18, 2009, released its Report on strengthening the forensic sciences in the United States. For an overall discussion of the report, see the discussion beginning on page 4 of this Supplement. As is by now well known among forensic science practitioners, the report was critical of several forensic disciplines, including firearm and toolmark examination evidence. Unlike our main text, the NAS Reports treats toolmark and firearms identification practices under the same general label and make no distinctions between the two.

The 2009 Report stressed that an earlier National Academies Report on *Ballistic Imaging*, had observed that the "validity of the fundamental assumptions of uniqueness and reproducibility of firearms-related toolmarks has not yet been fully demonstrated."[1] In its Summary to the firearm/toolmark discussions, the current NAS Report concluded:

> Toolmark and firearm analysis suffers from the same limitations discussed above for impression evidence. Because not enough is known about the variabilities among individual tools and guns, we are not able to specify how many points of similarity are necessary for a given level of confidence in the result. Sufficient studies have not been done to understand the reliability and repeatability of the methods. The committee agrees that class characteristics are helpful in narrowing the pool of tools that may have left a distinctive mark. Individual patterns from manufacture or from wear might, in some cases, be distinctive enough to suggest one particular source, but additional studies should be performed to make the process of individualization more precise and repeatable.

> A fundamental problem with toolmark and firearms analysis is the lack of a precisely defined process. As noted above, AFTE has adopted a theory of identification, but it does not provide a specific protocol.... This AFTE document, which is the best guidance

---

1. NAS Report, page 5–20.

available for the field of toolmark identification, does not even consider, let alone address, questions regarding variability, reliability, repeatability, or the number of correlations needed to achieve a given degree of confidence.

Although some studies have been performed on the degree of similarity that can be found by marks made by different tools and the variability in marks made by an individual tool, the scientific knowledge base for toolmark and firearm analysis is fairly limited. . . . [2]

§ 8.19   Cartridge Case Identification Evidence

Page 475, at the end of footnote 7, *add the following text*:

The *Green* holding was rejected in Commonwealth v. Meeks, 2006 WL 2819423 (Mass.Sup.Ct.2006), in a holding that permitted the examiner-witness to state not only his opinion of the outcome of the comparison, but also explain the reasons for it. Furthermore, the *Meeks* court stated that the cases weigh in favor of a finding that ballistics evidence is reliable.

§ 8.21   Bullet Lead Analysis Evidence

2.   POST–*DAUBERT/KUMHO TIRE* CASES

Page 478, at the end of footnote 9, *add the following text*:

In State v. Behn, 375 N.J.Super. 409, 868 A.2d 329 (2005), the appellate court similarly recognized the recent scientific studies that had questioned the validity of CBLA and concluded that the expert testimony adduced at Behn's first trial was "based on erroneous scientific foundations and its admission met the requirements for granting a new trial on the ground of newly discovered evidence."

VIII.   MISCELLANEOUS

§ 8.32   Bibliography of Additional References

Page 511, at the beginning of this section, *insert the following additional text and sources*:

Extensive discussions on firearm examination, toolmark comparisons, and other issues discussed in this chapter are contained in the recently published Wiley Encyclopedia of Forensic Science. In its 5 volumes, published in 2009, can be found a number of extensively annotated articles on the topics covered in this chapter, by prominent authorities in the field who offer a world-wide perspective on their topics. The print version of this reference work is due to be updated annually online, which updates will be made available by subscription. A few of the significant contributions to the literature and science relative

---

2. NAS Report, page 5–21. Where the Report refers to AFTE in the second quoted paragraph, the bases for conclusions by that organization were set out above, at page 43 of this Supplement, in the added material under § 8.08 of the main text.

to firearm and toolmark examinations to be found in the Encyclopedia are listed herein in this Supplement, infra, in § 8.23.

Christina S. Atwater, Marie E. Durina, & Robert D. Blackledge, "Visualization of Gunshot Residue Patterns on Dark Clothing using the Video Spectral Comparator," 51 J. FORENSIC SCIENCES 1091 (2006).

Donald E. Carlucci, *Ballistics—Theory and Design of Guns and Ammunition*, CRC PRESS, 2007.

Clare H. Cunliffe & J. Scott Denton, "An Atypical Gunshot Wound from a Home–Made Zip Gun—The Value of a Thorough Scene Investigation," 53 J. FORENSIC SCIENCES 216 (2008).

Gerard Dutton, "Firearms: Bullet and Cartridge Case Identification," in WILEY ENCYCLOPEDIA OF FORENSIC SCIENCE (Jamieson, A. & Moenssens, A.A., eds.) 2009 [3] 1204.

Dale Garrison, "Comparison Question: Should Photographic Documentation Be a Standard Operating Procedure for all Firearm and Toolmark Examinations?" EVIDENCE TECHNOLOGY MAGAZINE, Nov.-Dec. 2007, p. 12.

Paul C. Giannelli, "Comparative Bullet Lead Analysis—An Update," CRIMINAL JUSTICE, Summer 2008, p. 24.

John Gibeaut, "A Shot at the Second Amendment," ABA J., Nov. 2007, p. 50.

H. W. Hendrick, P. Paradis & R.J. Hornick, *Human Factors Issues in Handgun Safety and Forensics,* CRC PRESS, 2008.

Horst Katterwe, "Toolmarks," in WILEY ENCYCLOPEDIA OF FORENSIC SCIENCE (Jamieson, A. & Moenssens, A.A., eds.) 2009 [5] 2485.

Gregory S. Klees, "How Today's Firearm and Toolmark Examiners Can Prepare for Admissibility Hearings," EVIDENCE TECHNOLOGY MAGAZINE, Nov.-Dec. 2007, p. 26.

Nicholas Maiden, "Firearms: Scene Investigation," in WILEY ENCYCLOPEDIA OF FORENSIC SCIENCE (Jamieson, A. & Moenssens, A.A., eds.) 2009 [3] 1219.

Nicholas Maiden, "Serial Number Restoration," in WILEY ENCYCLOPEDIA OF FORENSIC SCIENCE (Jamieson, A. & Moenssens, A.A., eds.) 2009 [3] 1204.

Ludwig Niewoeher et al. [6 co-authors], "GSR2005—Continuity of the ENFSI Proficiency Test on Identification of GSR by SEM/EDX," 53 J. FORENSIC SCIENCES 162 (2008).

Ronald Nichols, "The Scientific Foundations of Firearms and Tool Mark Identification—A Response to Recent Challenges," CAC NEWS, 2d Quarter 2006, p. 8.

Robald Nichols, "Defending the Scientific Foundations of the Firearms and Tool Mark Identification Discipline: Responding to Recent Challenges," 52 J. FORENSIC SCIENCES 586 (2007).

James Smyth Wallace, *Chemical Analysis of Firearms, Ammunition, and Gunshot Residue*, CRC Press, 2008.

Arie Zeichner, "Firearm Discharge Residue: Analysis Of," in WILEY ENCYCLOPEDIA OF FORENSIC SCIENCE (Jamieson, A. & Moenssens, A.A., eds.) 2009 [3] 1189.

Arie Zeichner, "Shooting Distance: Estimation of," in WILEY ENCYCLOPEDIA OF FORENSIC SCIENCE (Jamieson, A. & Moenssens, A.A., eds.) 2009 [5] 2351.

Chapter 9

FIRE SCENE AND EXPLOSIVES INVESTIGATION

II. BASICS OF FIRE SCENE AND EXPLOSIVES INVESTIGATIONS

§ 9.04 The Fundamentals of Fire

Page 528, line 2, at the end of the sentence and before the start of the first full paragraph, *insert the following footnote*:

The 5–volume WILEY ENCYCLOPEDIA OF FORENSIC SCIENCE, published in 2009, contains a number of extensively illustrated and annotated articles on topics covered in this chapter. Some are included in the supplemental entries for § 9.25, infra. In connection with this section's coverage of the fundamentals of fire, we recommend reading the article by John J. Lentini, "Fire: Chemistry of," in Wiley Encyclopedia of Forensic Science (Jamieson, A. & Moenssens, A.A., eds.) 2009 [3] 1103.

III. INVESTIGATIVE ASPECTS

§ 9.07 Expert Qualifications

Page 540, at the end of the second full paragraph, *insert the following new footnote*:

See also, John J. Lentini, "Fire Investigation: Standardization, Accreditation, and Certification," in WILEY ENCYCLOPEDIA OF FORENSIC SCIENCE (Jamieson, A. & Moenssens, A.A., eds.) [3] 1171 (2009).

IV. LABORATORY ANALYSIS

§ 9.11 Fire Scene Evidence

Page 555, in the first full paragraph, at the end of the first sentence (line 2), *insert the following additional footnote*:

For an extensively illustrated and annotated treatment of laboratory fire remains analysis, see John J. Lentini, "Fire Debris: Laboratory Analysis of," in WILEY ENCYCLOPEDIA OF FORENSIC SCIENCE (Jamieson, A. & Moenssens, A.A., eds.) 2009 [3] 1137.

V. EVIDENCE OF FIRE EVENTS AND EXPLOSIVES USE

§ 9.23   Expert Testimony

1.   CAUSE AND SITUS OR ORIGIN OF FIRE OR EXPLOSION

Page 604, at the end of the second full paragraph, *insert the following new footnote*:

In 2009, the National Academy of Science released its report titled "Strengthening Forensic Sciences in the United States," in which some forensic disciplines were soundly criticized for their use of either unvalidated methodologies or reliance on inadequately researched scientific postulates. While the discipline of fire and explosives investigations escaped harsh criticism, any opinion testimony given by expert witnesses may still be subjected to close scrutiny as to whether it comports with what the NAS Report sees as "good forensic practice." The Report's principal provisions were explored in some detail in this Supplement, in Chapter 1, beginning at p. 4. Fire and Explosives investigators are advised to become familiar with the report, since questioning in court may focus on some of the Report's recommendations.

VII.   MISCELLANEOUS

§ 9.25   Bibliography of Additional References

[Explanatory note: Although the main text separates the section into three different subsections, because of the limited number of additional entries, they are combined hereafter.—Editor.]

Page 609, beginning after the introductory "Note," *insert the following additional sources*:

Bruce A. Bucholz, "Bomb–Pulse Dating," in WILEY ENCYCLOPEDIA OF FORENSIC SCIENCE (Jamieson, A. & Moenssens, A.A., eds.), 2009 [1] 418.

Douglas J. Carpenter, "Fire Modeling and its Application in Fire Investigation," in WILEY ENCYCLOPEDIA OF FORENSIC SCIENCE (Jamieson, A. & Moenssens, A.A., eds.) 2009 [3] 1175.

James B. Crippin, *Explosives and Chemical and Weapons Identification,* CRC Press, 2006.

Rick Houghton, *Field Confirmation: Testing for Suspicious Substances,* CRC Press, 2009.

Raymond J. Kuk & Michael V. Spagnola, "Extraction of Alternative Fuels from Fire Debris Samples," 53 J. FORENSIC SCIENCE 1123 (2008).

John J. Lentini, "Fire: Scene Investigation," in WILEY ENCYCLOPEDIA OF FORENSIC SCIENCE (Jamieson, A. & Moenssens, A.A., eds.) 2009 [3] 1122.

Sarah L. Lancaster, Maurice Marshall & Jimmie C. Oxley, "Explosion Debris: Laboratory Analysis of," in WILEY ENCYCLOPEDIA OF FORENSIC SCIENCE (Jamieson, A. & Moenssens, A.A., eds.) 2009 [2] 1028.

R. M. Morgan, et al. [5 co-authors], "The Preservation of Quartz Grain Surface Following Vehicle Fire and Their Use in Forensic Enquiry," 48 SCIENCE AND JUSTICE 133 (2008).

Bronwyn C. Morrish et al. [6 co-authors], "Chemical, Biological, Radiological, and Nuclear Investigations," in WILEY ENCYCLOPEDIA OF FORENSIC SCIENCE (Jamieson, A. & Moenssens, A.A., eds.) 2009 [2] 500.

Keith Norman & Victoria Gillman, "Chemical Warfare Agents," in WILEY ENCYCLOPEDIA OF FORENSIC SCIENCE (Jamieson, A. & Moenssens, A.A., eds.) 2009 [3] 507.

Kwok Y. Ong, *Detection Technologies for Chemical Warfare Agents and Toxic Vapors,* CRC Press, 2005.

Jimmie C. Oxley, James L. Smith, Louis J. Kirschenbaum, Suvarna Marimganti, & Sravanthi Vadlamannati, "Detection of Explosives in Hair Using Ion Mobility Spectrometry," 53 J. FORENSIC SCIENCE 690 (2008).

Nicholas D. K. Patraco, Mark Gil, Peter A. Pizzola & T. A. Kubic, "Statistical Discrimination of Liquid Gasoline Samples from Casework," 53 J. FORENSIC SCIENCE 1092 (2008).

David Royds, "Bomb Scene Management," in WILEY ENCYCLOPEDIA OF FORENSIC SCIENCE (Jamieson, A. & Moenssens, A.A., eds.) 2009 [1] 411.

James J. Thurman, "Explosions: Scene Investigation," in WILEY ENCYCLOPEDIA OF FORENSIC SCIENCE (Jamieson, A. & Moenssens, A.A., eds.) 2009 [2] 1018.

Thomas Wampler, *Applied Pyrolysis Handbook*, 2nd ed., CRC Press, 2007.

Hiroaka Yoshida, Tsyoshi Kaneko & Shinichi Suzuki, "A Solid-phase Microextraction Method for the Detection of Ignitable Liquids in Fire Debris," 53 J. FORENSIC SCIENCES 668 (2008).

Chapter 10

FINGERPRINT IDENTIFICATION

———

I. INTRODUCTION

§ 10.01 Scope of the Chapter

Page 621. At the end of the first paragraph, *insert the following additional paragraph:*

As has been mentioned in this Supplement earlier,[1] the National Academy of Science, on February 18, 2009, released its Report titled Strengthening the Forensic Sciences in the United States. As is by now well known to most forensic practitioners and litigators, the report was critical of several forensic disciplines, among them the conducting of firearm and toolmark examinations. But no discipline, save perhaps the medical-legal investigation of death and its antiquated coroner system, was discussed as often as fingerprint identification. It was mentioned at least once in each of the report's Chapters 2 through 4, and extensively in Chapter 5. We will explore the relevance of the comments further on in the discussion of the current chapter.[2] It deserves mention at an early stage that fingerprint identification continues to be recognized as a respectable and reliable method of personal identification, providing a valuable contribution that is on a par with that of the DNA technique in assuring the appropriate functioning of the criminal justice system.

Nothing stated in the report invalidates the determinations of a "match," or the lack thereof, made after an experienced and trained examiner has made a comparison of known and unknown prints. Since the forensic sciences have progressed at an ever increasing rate during the last two decades, many applicable recommendations in the report that relate specifically to fingerprint identification were already part and parcel of current practices, guidelines, and standards in the profession.

§ 10.03 Definitions of Terms

Page 623. At the end of the first paragraph, and before the listing of definitions, *add the following additional paragraph:*

Over the past several years, SWGFAST has been reviewing its documents with the aim of improving and adapting them to keep pace

---

1. See, supra, page 4 of this Supplement. The report is referred to in this Supplement as the NAS Report or, alternatively, as the 2009 NAS Report.

2. See the new § 10.08–6, infra this Supplement.

with current advancements in the science. So it has been with its Glossary of definitions, which has gone through extensive review over the past two years. As a result, SWGFAST has adopted a significantly modified glossary which, under its charter, has now been posted for comment on its website[1] before it can become an official adopted standard. The modifications of definitions are not reflected in the current 2009 Supplement because they are not, as yet, in effect, and may be further revised after the expiration of the public comment period.

II. CLASSIFICATION AND USES OF FINGERPRINTS

§ 10.05   Fundamental Premises of Friction Ridge Individuality

Page 631. At the end of footnote 3, *add the following text:*

See also, Alice Maceo, "Friction Ridge Skin: Morphogenesis and Overview," in WILEY ENCYCLOPEDIA OF FORENSIC SCIENCE (Jamieson, A. & Moenssens, A.A., eds.) [3] 1322 (2009, for an full, extensively illustrated discussion of the process of prenatal friction ridge development).

§ 10.08   The Individualization ("Identification") of Friction Ridge Impressions

3.   THE ACE–V METHODOLOGY

a.   RENAMING RIDGE FEATURES ACCORDING TO LEVELS OF DETAIL

Page 648. After the end mention of footnote 7 in the second full paragraph, *insert the following additional sentences into the main text:*

Recent research conducted by noted fingerprint researchers at the Forensic Science Service in the U.K. and at *the Ecole des Sciences Criminelles, Institut de Police Scientifique* of the University of Lausanne, Switzerland, found that there was no clear consensus among practitioners, mostly from the U.S., on which characteristics are to be designated as belonging to the Level 3 category.[1] Nor was there agreement on the reproducibility and individual value of such detail.

Ridge edges and pores were generally recognized as belonging in the Level 3 category, as were width of ridges and furrows. Less agreement existed with regard to incipient ridges and dots. Detail such as creases, warts, and scars elicited less acceptance as potential Level 3 detail, though nearly all of the practitioners surveyed gave them great individualizing importance. While this might suggest additional agreement with-

---

1. www.swgfast.org under Drafts for Comments.

1. Alexandre Anthonioz, Nicole Egli, Christophe Champod, Cedric Neumann, Roberto Puch–Solis & Andie Bromage–Griffiths, "Level 3 Details and Their Role in Fingerprint Identification: A Survey among Practitioners," 5 J. OF FORENSIC IDENTIFICATION 562 (2008).

in the profession about the nature of Level 3 Detail is desirable, it may suggest that moving away from reliance on "features." The research findings do not invalidate reliance on such detail in making an identification

4.   FURTHER RESEARCH

Page 651. At the end of the subsection, *insert the following additional text:*

Despite budgetary limitations, research is continuing at an accelerating pace. Enlisting the aid of academics, fingerprint practitioners have initiated research proposals on a variety of subjects. Interactions with DNA techniques have been explored, and the question of whether DNA may be used to identify an individual through the perspiration in a latent impression.[2] The development of statistical modeling and the development of likelihood ratios to support identification decisions continues to be considered with greater intensity.[3] Research on the effects of bias of various sorts, and to what extend it may lead to erroneous identifications, is also continuing. Behaviorists are also exploring how a fingerprint examiner processes information that may lead to decision making.[4]

Page 652. At the end of current § 10.08, *insert the following new subsection:*

6.   THE 2009 NATIONAL ACADEMY OF SCIENCE (NAS) REPORT

As indicated earlier,[5] the NAS Report singled out fingerprint identification for repeated references. Beginning in Chapter 2, it states that fingerprint examinations "may be conducted by sworn law enforcement officers with no scientific training."[6]

2. E.g., Jennifer J. Raymond, Claude Roux & Simon J. Walsh, "Friction Ridge Skin—Interaction between Fingerprint Detection and DNA/Biological Material," in WILEY ENCYCLOPEDIA OF FORENSIC SCIENCE (Jamieson, A. & Moenssens, A.A., eds.) 2009 [3] 1318.

The suggestion made, several years ago, that DNA might make fingerprint searches obsolete and that latent fingerprint traces would, in the future, be analyzed solely by the DNA contained in perspiration, is unlikely to occur. Not only is it common for perspiration to be of insufficient quantity and quality for preservation and analysis by biological methods, but current DNA research has also determined that cross-contamination of one person's DNA upon another's biological material is so common that it may confound accurate attributions as to origin.

3. Dr. Christophe Champod, an indefatigeable researcher in forensic decision making, explores and annotates the various modern statistical models that are publish-

ed in the peer review literature, in: Christophe Champod, "Friction Ridge Examination (Fingerprints): Interpretation of," in WILEY ENCYCLOPEDIA OF FORENSIC SCIENCE (Jamieson, A. & Moenssens, A.A., eds.) 2009 [3] 1277. See also, Cedric Neumann, Christophe Champod, Roberto Puch–Solis, Nicole Egli, Alexandre Antonioz & Andie Bromage–Griffiths, "Computation of Likelihood Ratios in Fingerprint Identification for Configurations of Any Number of Minutiae," 52 J. FORENSIC SCIENCE 54 (2007).

4. Thomas A. Busey & John Vanderkolk, "Behavioral and Electrophysiological Evidence for Configural Processing in Fingerprint Experts," 45 VISION RESEARCH 431 (2005).

5. Supra page 4 of this Supplement, and in the text at footnote 1, herein.

6. NAS Report, p. 2–3. No mention is made of the tendency to replace identification workers in local departments with science-trained civilians, not that possession of

In Chapter 3, repeated references are made that may be read as impugning the validity of fingerprint individualizations.[7] In the same chapter, the report critiques federal appeals court decisions that found fingerprinting to meet *Daubert* factors, contrasting that to the widely publicized Brandon Mayfield misidentification[8] as well as a recent non-reviewable single judge's pretrial decision to bar fingerprint opinions as to the significance of a match.[9] The Brandon Mayfield case is mentioned again in Chapter 4 as the legitimate example of how bias may affect decision making.[10]

It is in Chapter 5 of the report that the main thrust of the critical evaluation is contained. After extolling the presumed superiority of DNA analysis as "the" standard against which the report's authors judged all forensic science,[11] the report begins its examination of fingerprints. The initial few pages describe the uses of fingerprints, the professional societies to which most identification examiners belong, and the guideline/standard-setting function of SWGFAST. The ACE–V method is also explained, though for its more detailed description, the readers are referred to a paper by two is also explained, though for its more detailed description, the readers are referred to a paper by two frequent critics who are not-fingerprint examiners.[12]

In its discussion of Methods of Interpretation, the report recognizes that the determination of an exclusion is recognized as often being "straightforward." The same may be said for 10–print fingerprint cards, but the report exhibits a reluctance to endorse to the same extent single latent impression comparisons because of he absence of a sufficient number of population statistics as to the frequency with which certain characteristics may appear in latent impressions that are fragmentary.

The main basis for the report's criticism is in the range of conclusions permitted under common practice. It recognizes that SWGFAST specifies three acceptable conclusions after comparing a latent to a

undergraduate degrees is becoming the norm for employment and examiner certification.

7. NAS Report, p. 3, vaunting the superiority of DNA analysis among the forensic methods of "individualizing" evidence, and at p. 10, critiquing a 7th Circuit Court of Appeals decision that gave unqualified approval to fingerprinting as that was "straining scientific credulity for the sake of a venerable forensic science" (the quote is from a law professor's book).

8. NAS Report, pp. 3–14 to 16. The report makes no mention of procedural changes placed in effect in the affected agency (the FBI) and in the profession generally in the aftermath of this erroneous attribution to prevent similar recurrences.

9. State v. Rose, Case No. K–06–0545 (Circuit Court for Baltimore Co., Oct. 19, 2007). In a similar later case in Howard County, the court specifically rejected the Rose rationale and permitted the expert to testify to a conclusion, stating, "the fact that a procedure or process could be improved does not entitle the Court to bar the current examiners from providing testimony that would be useful to the trier of fact. The perfect should not become the enemy of the good." State v. Johnson, Case No. 13–K–07–47108 (Circuit Court for Howard County, March 26, 2008).

10. NAS Report, p. 4–10.

11. NAS Report, pp. 3, 5. Controlled substances analysis is also seen as a "mature" forensic discipline because of its reliance on classical analytical chemistry methods.

12. L. Haber & R. N. Haber, "Scientific Validation of Fingerprint Evidence under *Daubert*," 7 LAW, PROBABILITY AND RISK 87 (2008).

known print: individualization (identification), exclusion, or inconclusive. While the report accurately recognizes that the decision of identification includes a "subjective assessment" of a number of factors, it inaccurately equates opinion testimony that an individualization exists to the professing of "absolute certainty" as a factual assertion, rather than as an opinion.[13] If that were the case, such claim would indeed be insupportable in science. But while some older examiners may have either expressed absolute certainty in their conclusions, or through lack of testimonial precision may have been misunderstood as asserting this as a fact rather than an opinion, the trend has long been away from making such categorical statements as existing fact.

No matter how understood, the conclusion reached by an examiner after comparing known and unknown prints represents that examiner's opinion. The examiner expresses an opinion on the basis of experience and training, and that opinion may include the personal conviction that the likelihood of finding the same ridge detail in agreement between impressions made by different individuals, though theoretically possible, is so remote that the examiner is willing to ignore it and consider the match as "positive." But it remains the examiner's opinion, and not a scientific fact. More and more examiners, who are increasingly being trained in science as well, are being instructed to better articulate the nature of their findings.

Chapter 5 also stresses the need for appropriate documentation citing a court decision wherein documentation of the analysis process had not been affected, but does not mention the fact the court determined that the absence of appropriate documentation does not mean the identification was in error.[14] In any event, the report fails to mention that extensive documentation is currently required under ASCLD–LAB, as well as in many local laboratories, and that SWGFAST has developed a standard mandating appropriate documentation and describing its extent in considerable detail.

The report does admit, apparently grudgingly, that "Some scientific evidence supports the presumption that friction ridge patterns are unique to each person and remain unchanged throughout a lifetime."[15] But it recommends additional research be done—research tied to a statistical approach—which "could provide examiners with a more robust understanding of the prevalence of different ridge flows and crease patterns."[16] The report recognizes that such research has been and is being conducted.

In all, far from suggesting that fingerprints are unreliable forms of identification, as some media articles had suggested, the report is affirmative of the technique and makes suggestions were additional research or the imposition of stricter standards—both of which have been advo-

13. NAS Report, p. 5–12.   **15.** Id.

14. NAS Report, p. 5–13.   **16.** Ibid.

cated repeatedly by leaders in the profession—can strengthen forensic science in the United States.

In its separate Chapter 10, the Report addresses needed research designed to remedy interoperability problems with automated identification systems.[17] The proliferation of systems produced by different vendors may pose problems of connecting a specific case to data already on file elsewhere. Most of the problems are technical ones, on which research the American National Standards Institute (ANSI), the National Institute of Standards and Technology (NIST), as well as state and federal law enforcement agencies worldwide have been working for several years.[18] As incremental improvements are made, the potential of the system keeps growing.

III. FINGERPRINTS AS EVIDENCE

§ 10.09 Admissibility in Evidence of Fingerprint Comparisons

2. POST *DAUBERT* APPROACH TO PROVING DEFENDANT'S IDENTITY

a. FEDERAL CASES

Page 660. At the end of footnote 40, *add the following decisions:*

United States v. Vargas, 471 F.3d 255 (1st Cir.2006), wherein the expert was cross-examined on all of the *Daubert* factors as they relate to fingerprinting-expert testimony constituted a reliable application of fingerprint analysis to the facts of the case even though the expert failed to provide documentation of his analysis; United States v. Estrada, 453 F.3d 1208 (9th Cir. 2006).

b. STATE CASES

Page 663. At the end of the subsection, and before Proof of Victim's Identity, *insert the following text:*

Significant also is the 2008 decision of State v. Langill,[1] in which the New Hampshire Supreme Court upheld the use of fingerprint identification testimony. The case involved a single fingerprint that tied defendant to a burglary. Prior to trial, a *Daubert* hearing had been held after which the trial judge excluded the evidence of the fingerprint comparison, finding there was simply not enough information to support a finding that the ACE–V methodology was properly applied in the case. Further-

---

17. NAS Report, pp. 10–1 through 7.

18. See, e.g., Laura Hutchins, "What the Future Can Hold: A Look at the Connectivity of Automated Fingerprint Identification Systems," 59 J. FORENSIC IDENTIFICATION 275 (2009); Didier Meuwly, "Automated Fingerprint Identification Systems (AFIS)" in WILEY ENCYCLOPEDIA OF FORENSIC SCIENCE (Jamieson, A. & Moenssens, A.A., eds.) [1] 249 (2009); Kristi Mayo, "AFIS Interoperability," Evidence Technology Mag., Jan.-Feb. 2008, p. 12.

1. 157 N.H. 77, 945 A.2d 1 (2008). http://www.nh.gov/judiciary/supreme/opinions/langi032.pdf.

more, the judge asserted that the examiner failed to memorialize how the ACE–V protocols were adhered to. No "bench notes" (documentation) of the analysis and comparison had been recorded apart from the photographs taken that contain the observed characteristics, and no blind verification had been performed since such procedure was not required by departmental protocols.

The State appealed the pre-trial order, arguing that the trial court exceeded its discretion by making a threshold determination of inadmissibility, imposing on the examiner standards of reliability beyond those approved or required by the scientific community. In so doing, it was argued, the judge usurped the jury's function of weighing the credibility of the expert's testimony.

A unanimous New Hampshire Supreme Court reversed the order excluding the expert's opinion evidence and remanded the case for trial. Even if the examiner failed to document the application of the ACE–V method—a process that was not required at that time in most state jurisdictions in the United States or in Canada, though maintaining appropriate documentation may become the norm in the future—that did not render inadmissible the expert's opinion resulting from her comparison. The Supreme Court stated that the decision of whether the expert properly applied the ACE–V method belonged in the hands of the jury, after direct testimony and cross-examination by the defense.

After examining the *Daubert* standard of reliability, which had been adopted as part of state law in New Hampshire, the court decided that in an evidentiary context, "reliable" does not mandate correctness. The purpose of the rule is simply to ensure that the jury is presented with reliable and relevant evidence, not flawless evidence. On the issue of lack of blind verification, the court added:

> While we acknowledge that a small number of misidentification cases using ACE–V methodology do exist, it is undisputed that ACE–V methodology has been reliably applied in countless cases without the use of blind verification. Further, as the testimony of [defense witness James] Starrs and [prosecution witness Steven] Ostrowski demonstrates, the fingerprint community is currently debating whether blind verification actually leads to more accurate results To be sure, while blind verification may ensure with a higher level of certainty that an identification is correct, the record contains no indication that non-blind verification is unreliable.[2]

The court also recognized—as had the defense expert—that blind verification "is a new thing entirely" and not currently widely seen as required.

§ 10.11 Expert Qualifications

Page 678. At the end of footnote 9, *add the following text:*

The re-certification requirements for certified latent print examiners were changed again during 2007, the changes to take effect on Jan. 1, 2008. The fairly lengthy

2. Id. at ___.

revised changes are described in, Kasey Wertheim, "New 2008 IAI Re–Certification Requirements," in Detail #312 (Aug. 2007) published on www.clpex.com.

———

V. TRIAL PRACTICE

§ 10.20 Bibliography

On Page 701. Beginning after the introductory sentence to the section, *insert the following additional materials:*

1. BOOKS

Mark Hawthorne, *Fingerprints—Analysis and Understanding*, CRC Press, 2008.

2. ARTICLES

Shaheen Aumeer–Donovan, Chris Lennard & Claude Roux, "Friction Ridge Skin: Fingerprint Detection and Recovery Techniques," in WILEY ENCYCLOPEDIA OF FORENSIC SCIENCE (Jamieson, A. & Moenssens, A.A., eds.) 2009 [3] 1292.

G. Bradshaw, S. Bleah, J. Deans & N. NicDaeid, "Recovery of Fingerprints from Arson Scenes: Latent Fingerprints," FINGERPRINT WHORLD, Jan. 2009, www.fpsociety.org.

Christophe Champod, "Friction Ridge Examination (Identification): Interpretation of," in WILEY ENCYCLOPEDIA OF FORENSIC SCIENCE (Jamieson, A. & Moenssens, A.A., eds.) 2009 [3] 1277.

David Charlton, Peter A. F. Frazer–Mackenzie & Itiel E. Dror, "Emotional Experiences and Motivating Factors Associated with Fingerprint Analysis," In Press, J. FORENSIC SCIENCES, received from david. charlton97@btinternet.com.

Kerri Huss, John "Dusty" Clark & W. Jerry Chisum, "Which Was First—Fingerprint or Blood," 50 J. FORENSIC IDENTIFICATION 344 (2000).

Anil K. Jain & Sharath Pankanti, "Beyond Fingerprinting," SCIENTIFIC AMERICAN, Sep. 2008, p. 78.

O. P. Jasuja, Gagan Deep Singh & G. S. Sodhi, "Small Particle Reagents: Development of Fluorescent Variants," 48 SCIENCE AND JUSTICE 141 (2008).

Glenn Langenburg, "Friction Ridge Skin: Comparison and Identification," in WILEY ENCYCLOPEDIA OF FORENSIC SCIENCE (Jamieson, A. & Moenssens, A.A., eds.) 2009 [3] 1282.

Tony B. P. Larkin, Nicholas P. Marsh & Patricia M. Larrigan, "Using Liquid Latex to Remove Soot to Facilitate Fingerprint and Bloodstain Examinations: A Case Study," 58 J. OF FORENSIC IDENTIFICATION 540 (2008).

Tony Larkin & Chris Ganniliffe 3, "Illuminating The Health and Safety of Luminol," 48 SCIENCE AND JUSTICE 71 (2008).

John Lewis Larson, "Prints From Skin," EVIDENCE TECHNOLOGY MAG., May–June 2008, p. 18.

Simon W. Lewis & Felippo Barni, "Luminol," in WILEY ENCYCLOPEDIA OF FORENSIC SCIENCE (Jamieson, A. & Moenssens, A.A., eds.) 2009 [3] 1645.

Fang Li, "Probability of False Positive with an Innocent Image Processing Routine," 58 J. FORENSIC IDENTIFICATION 551 (2008).

Alice V. Maceo, "Friction Ridge Skin: Morphogenesis and Overview," in WILEY ENCYCLOPEDIA OF FORENSIC SCIENCE (Jamieson, A. & Moenssens, A.A., eds.) 2009 [3] 1322.

Jaroslaw Moszczynski, Antoni Siejca & Llukasz Ziemnicki, "New System for the Acquisition of Fingerprints by Means of Time–Resolved Luminescence," 58 J. FORENSIC IDENTIFICATION 515 (2008).

Steven L. Petersen, Shawn L. Naccarato & Gary John, "Enhancing Latent Prints," FORENSIC MAGAZINE, Dec. 2007, p. 31.

Andrew D. Reinholz, "Albumin Development Method to Visualize Friction Ridge Detail on Porous Surfaces," 58 J. FORENSIC IDENTIFICATION 524 (2008).

Michelle Triplett, "Fingerprint Competency," EVIDENCE TECHNOLOGY MAG., March–April 2008, p. 30.

Stephen P. Wargacki, Linda A. Lewis & Mark D. Dadmun, "Enhancing the Quality of Aged Latent Fingerprints Developed by Superglue Fuming: Loss and Replenishment of Initiator," 53 J. FORENSIC SCIENCES 1138 (2008).

Pat A. Wertheim, "Fingerprint Forgery: A Case Study," IDENTIFICATION NEWS Vol. 38, No. 6, p. 12 (2008).

Chapter 11

TRACE EVIDENCE—THE SOURCE IDENTIFI-
CATION AND COMPARISON OF SMALL
OBJECTS AND PARTICLES

I. INTRODUCTION

§ 11.01 Scope of the Chapter

Page 709. At the end of the section (bottom of the page) *insert the following new material*:

THE 2009 NATIONAL ACADEMY OF SCIENCES
(NAS) REPORT ON FORENSIC SCIENCE

As indicated elsewhere,[1] during the early part of 2009, a committee of the National Academy of Science released a report titled: Strengthening Forensic Sciences in he United States—A Path Forward. Since the report discussed the needs of the professional community in several disciplines, in addition to the general discussion that commences in Chapter 1, we have made and continue to make, references to the report in other chapters as well.

The group of specialties that is loosely classified under the designation "Trace Evidence Examination" in this chapter fared much better, in the way of criticism as some other disciplines did. Perhaps that was due to the fact that, in Trace Evidence, the result of a technical or scientific examination is seldom reported as a match/no-match outcome. Instead, use of a terminology in reports and when testifying in court that couches conclusions regarding the significance of findings more tentatively. They are often expressed in degrees of probability.

In its organization of Chapter 5 of the report, biological evidence is first to be discussed, followed by the analysis of controlled substances and friction ridge analysis (fingerprints). It is not until then that the report reaches the topic of "Other Pattern/Impression Evidence."

With regard to this chapter's subject matter the report discusses briefly the topics of shoeprints and tire tracks, hair examinations, fiber investigations, and paint coatings, and makes casual mention, without elaboration, of several other types of pattern evidence. The report stresses that there is a long lis of potential types of impression evidence

---

1. The 2009 NAS Report, see p. 4 this Supplement, supra, hereafter referred to as NAS Report, the 2009 NAS Report or, simply, the report.

that might also be considered, such as bite marks, firearm and ammunition evidence, ear prints, lip prints, tool markings, bloodstain patterns, as well as glove prints. Some of these topics are covered in different chapters of the main text.

1. SHOEPRINTS AND TIRE TRACKS

Among "Other Pattern/Impression Evidence," shoeprints and tire track evidence are mentioned first.[2] The various steps in the comparison process are recognized, beginning with an examination of class (or group) characteristics, after which it is sometimes possible to locate and compare individual characteristics, which are sometimes also referred to a accidental or random markings.

The report mentions that mass-produced items, such as shoes and tires, acquire features of wear or damage that often can be used to individualize them. Since the variability of class and individual characteristics is not known, workers in the field have not adopted a specific minimum number of matching characteristics that must be present in two samples that are compared, nor have they adopted a standard report terminology. The report references that some professionals follow recommended practices as set out by SWGTREAD, an FBI-sponsored group composed of footwear and tire track examiners:

> SWGTREAD, [composed of footwear and tire track examiners] recommends terminology such as:
>
> "identification" (definite conclusion of identity)
>
> "probably made" (very high degree of association)
>
> "could have made" (significant association of multiple class characteristics)
>
> "inconclusive" (limited association of some characteristics)
>
> "probably did not make" (very high degree of nonassociation)
>
> "elimination" (definite exclusion)
>
> "unsuitable" (lacks sufficient detail for a meaningful comparison)[3]

As for most evidence comparisons, the report deplores that the groups that work in the field, while moving toward standardization of terminology, do not address "the issue of what critical research should be done or by whom," nor do they stress the critical questions that should be answered

> "include the persistence of individual characteristics, the rarity of certain characteristic types, and he appropriate statistical standards to apply to the significance of individual characteristics. Also, little if any research has been done to address rare impression evidence. Much more research on these matters is needed."[4]

2. 2009 NAS Report, supra page 4 this Supplement, at 5–14.

3. 2009 NAS Report, supra page 4 this Supplement, at 5–17.

4. 2009 NAS Report, referred to supra at page 4, pages 5–18 & 5–18.

2. HAIR EXAMINATIONS

The 4+-page hair comparison treatment in the report discusses hair comparisons solely in the context of the microscopic analytical method.[5] It did not specifically address mitochondrial DNA or nuclear DNA practices in the examination of hair specimen. It summarized the significance of hair examinations in the section's first paragraph:

> The results of analyses from hair comparisons typically are accepted as class associations; that is, a conclusion of a "match" means only that the hair could have come from any person whose hair exhibited—within some levels of measurement uncertainties—the same microscopic characteristics, but it cannot uniquely identify one person. However, this information might be sufficiently useful to "narrow the pool" by excluding certain persons as sources of the hair.

After discussing briefly a method of examination and the classification of characteristics in categories of "major" and "minor" characteristics, the report turns to studies it described as dealing with the "accuracy of an identification," though it encompassed basically some probability calculation studies that have appeared in the journals. These were also discussed in our main text.[6] The report exhibits the same skepticism toward these studies as were reflected in our own chapter. In that regard, the report recognized that, while microscopic hair examinations are still conducted, their importance has lessened significantly after DNA and mtDNA examinations became generally available.[7]

3. FIBER COMPARISONS

The report's treatment of fiber examinations comprises less than two pages, and involves mainly a recognition that there are as yet no accepted standards on "the number and quality of characteristics that must correspond in order to conclude that two fibers came from the same manufacturing batch."[8] Thus, an association between a fiber and a suspected source only permits determining a possible origin.

The practice of fiber examination is recognized in the report as being based on "well-characterized methods of chemistry" and therefore capable of calculating the uncertainties inherent in an association, though such studies have not been done to date.

5. 2009 NAS Report, supra page 4. The discussion begins at p. 5–22.

6. Scientific Evidence in Civil and Criminal Identification, 5th ed., 2007, at p. 732 in § 11.13.

7. Hair cannot be individualized reliably, except by nuclear DNA of cell material adhering to hair roots of specimens that have been forcibly pulled out. Even though mitochondrial DNA also cannot individualize a specimen as originating from a specific source, mtDNA examinations will still narrow down the possibilities of inclusion to a far greater degree than is possible with microscopic examinations. See, main text at p. 732.

8. NAS Report, supra, at p. 5–27.

The report found that the results of an examination are reproducible across laboratories precisely because of the use of standard examination techniques.

4. PAINT AND COATINGS EVIDENCE

The analysis of paint and coatings evidence merited approx. three pages of the report.[9] The examination of paint and coatings permits a ready determination of certain class characteristics which tend to be replicable, in that they are based on well-known chemical analytical methods. It was stressed that there exist no agreed terminology in the manner in which findings are expressed. Thus, examination reports use a variety of conclusions, such as: "match," "indistinguishable from," "consistent with," or "similar" along with the properties detected in the paint samples compared. It recognizes that where multiple layers of paint coatings in a single sample exhibit similar characteristics, the significance of a "similar to" finding increases the evidentiary value of the opinion, though no definitive association to a specific source is possible.

Significantly, the report recognizes, as it did in regard to fibers, the guidelines for analysis set out by the FBI's SWGMAT, but stresses that although a range of possible conclusions can explain the significance of evidence that results from an examination, there are no criteria for determining a conclusion.

III. EXAMINATION OF HAIR

§ 11.13 Probabilities, Statistics, and Hair Comparisons

Page 734. At the end of footnote 5, *add the following text*:

For a discussion of probabilities in hair comparisons contained in the 2009 National Academy of Science Report, see supra p. 13 footnote 42 this Supplement.

IV. FIBERS

§ 11.18 Examination of Fibers

Page 746. At the end of the section, *insert the following new footnote*:

10. For a discussion of probabilities in fiber examinations contained in the 2009 National Academy of Science Report, see supra p. 13 at footnote 42 this Supplement.

---

9. NAS Report, supra, at p. 5–30.

V. PAINT

§ 11.22 Paint Examination Methods

Page 755. At the bottom of the page (the end of the section), *insert the following new footnote*:

2. For a discussion of paint comparisons contained in the 2009 National Academy of Science Report, see supra p. 13 this Supplement.

VII. MISCELLANEOUS PARTICLES

§ 11.31 Other Identification Methods Based on Various Types of Trace Evidence

1. ATTEMPTS TO INDIVIDUALIZE PERSONS BY THEIR LIP IMPRESSIONS

Page 770. At the end of the second full paragraph, *insert the following new footnote*:

8a. The 2009 National Academy of Science report did not specifically examine lip print evidence, though it made a casual mention of it in its discussion on "Other Impression/Pattern Evidence—Shoewear and Tire Impressions" when it said, at p. 5–17, "it is difficult to assert that the field has enough collective judgment about the variabilities in lip prints and ear prints based on tens of examinations."

2. ATTEMPTS TO INDIVIDUALIZE PERSONS BY THEIR EAR IMPRESSIONS

Page 772. At the end of footnote 14, *insert the following additional text*:

The 2009 National Academy of Science report did not explore the validity of ear impressions but remarked, at p. 5–17, "it is difficult to assert that the field has enough collective judgment about the variabilities in lip prints and ear prints based on tens of examinations." An attempt to combine probabilistic computer models to the comparison of ear impressions produced inconclusive, though encouraging results. See, Lynn Meijerman, A. Thean & G. J. R. Maat, "Earprints: Interpretation of," in WILEY ENCYCLOPEDIA OF FORENSIC SCIENCE (Jamieson, A. & Moenssens, A.A., eds.) 2009 [2] 891.

Page 774. After the end of the second line (and before the first full paragraph), *insert the following additional paragraph*:

The issue of earprint evidence came up again in a 2008 decision in the (U.K.) Court of Appeals.[1] A latent ear mark had been discovered during the investigation of a burglary scene, but the testimony of a fingerprint examiner that the ear print matched the known print of the defendant was not objected to initially. Relying partly on the Dallagher holding,[2] the defendant subsequently sought to purse a new appeal, as a result of which a conviction which conceivably might have been influenced by the ear print testimony was found the be "unsafe," and therefore reversed.

1. R. v. Kempster, [2008] EWCA Crim 975.

2. See discussion of the case on p. 773 of the main text.

The Court of Appeal, Criminal Division, said: "On the basis of the evidence that we have heard, we are of the view that the ... [ear-print comparison is capable of providing information which could identify the person who has left an ear-print on a surface, but that] can only be the case where the gross features truly provide a precise match.... But having examined the comparisons of the gross features, it is also apparent to us that they do not provide a precise match. The differences may well be explicable ... but the extent of the mismatch is such as to lead us to the conclusion that it could not be relied on by itself as justifying a verdict of guilty."[3]

————

IX. MISCELLANEOUS

§ 11.34 Bibliography of Additional References

Page 782. *Insert the following selected references:*

1. GENERAL ANALYTICAL PROCEDURES

Jihad Rene Albani, *Principles and Applications of Fluorescence Spectroscopy*, 2007.

Imran Ali & Hassan Y. Aboul–Enein, *Instrumental Methods in Metal Ion Speciation*, 2006.

Robert D. Blackledge, "The Increasingly Diverse and Challenging Discipline of Trace–Evidence Analysis," EVIDENCE TECHNOLOGY MAG., Nov.–Dec. 2008, p. 15.

M. J. Bogusz, *Forensic Science, Handbook of Analytical Separations*, 2008.

Richard G. Brereton, *Applied Chemometrics for Scientists*, 2007.

Chhabil Dass, *Fundamentals of Contemporary Mass Spectrometry*, 2007.

Peter R. Griffiths, *Fourier Transform, Infrared Spectrometry*, 2nd ed. 2007.

Eli Grushka & Nelu Grinberg, eds., *Advances in Chromatography*, 2007.

Thomas G. Hopen & Malcolm Davis, "Microscopy: Light Microscopes," in WILEY ENCYCLOPEDIA OF FORENSIC SCIENCE (Jamieson, A. & Moenssens, A.A., eds.) 2009 [4] 1762.

Rick Houghton, *Emergency Characterization of Unknown Materials*, 2008.

Aita Khanmy–Vidal, "Microscopy: Scanning Electron Microscopy," in WILEY ENCYCLOPEDIA OF FORENSIC SCIENCE (Jamieson, A. & Moenssens, A.A., eds.) 2009 [4] 1793.

---

3. Paragraph 28 of the Court's opinion.

K. Paul Kirkbride, "Microscopy: FTIR," in WILEY ENCYCLOPEDIA OF FORENSIC SCIENCE (Jamieson, A. & Moenssens, A.A., eds.) 2009 [4] 1750.

Teresa Kowalski & Joseph Sherma, *Preparative Layer Chromatography*, 2006.

Jorg P. Kutter & Yolanda Fintschenko, eds., *Separation Methods in Microanalytical Systems*, 2006.

Mary Giblin, "Sampling and Estimation of Quantities," in WILEY ENCYCLOPEDIA OF FORENSIC SCIENCE (Jamieson, A. & Moenssens, A.A., eds.) 2009 [5] 2283.

W. Roy Masson, *A Practical Guide to Magnetic Circular Dichroism Spectroscopy*, 2007.

Gilliam McMahon, *Analytical Instrumentation*, 2008.

Sean McDermott, "Trace Evidence: Transfer, Persistence, and Value," in WILEY ENCYCLOPEDIA OF FORENSIC SCIENCE (Jamieson, A. & Moenssens, A.A., eds.) 2009 [5] 2534.

Wilfried M. A. Niessen, *Liquid Chromatography—Mass Spectrometry*, 3rd ed., 2007.

Matthias Otto, *Chemometrics*, 2nd ed. 2007.

Elizabeth Prichard & Victoria Barwick, *Quality Assurance in Analytical Chemistry*, 2007.

James Robertson, "Microscopy: High Power," in WILEY ENCYCLOPEDIA OF FORENSIC SCIENCE (Jamieson, A. & Moenssens, A.A., eds.) 2009 [4] 1758.

James Robertson, "Microscopy: Low Power," in WILEY ENCYCLOPEDIA OF FORENSIC SCIENCE (Jamieson, A. & Moenssens, A.A., eds.) 2009 [4] 1791.

Dean Rood *The Troubleshooting and Maintenance Guide for Gas Chromatographers*, 4th ed., 2007.

William M. Schneck, "Microchemistry," in WILEY ENCYCLOPEDIA OF FORENSIC SCIENCE (Jamieson, A. & Moenssens, A.A., eds.) 2009 [4] 1743.

William M. Schneck, "Particles: Form," in WILEY ENCYCLOPEDIA OF FORENSIC SCIENCE (Jamieson, A. & Moenssens, A.A., eds.) 2009 [4] 2001.

Jennette M. Van Emon, *Immunoassay and other Bioanalytical Techniques*, 2007.

J. Trock Watson, *Introduction to Mass Spectrometry*, 2007.

Paul Yates, *Chemical Calculations*, 2nd ed., 2007.

3. HAIRS

Cary T. Oien, "Forensic Fair Comparison: Background Information for Interpretation," FORENSIC SCIENCE COMMUNICATIONS, 2009 [11]. Available at http://www.fbi.gov./hq/lab/fsc/current/review/2009, last visited on April 24, 2009.

Pascal Kintz, "Hair: Toxicology," in Wiley Encyclopedia of Forensic Science (Jamieson, A. & Moenssens, A.A., eds.) 2009 [3] 1427.

Sean McDermott, "Trace Evidence–Transfer and Persistence," in Wiley Encyclopedia of Forensic Science (Jamieson, A. & Moenssens, A.A., eds.) 2009 [5] 2534.

James Robertson, "Hair: Microscopic Analysis," in Wiley Encyclopedia of Forensic Science (Jamieson, A. & Moenssens, A.A., eds.) 2009 [3] 1415.

Silvana R. Tridico, "Hair: Animal," in Wiley Encyclopedia of Forensic Science (Jamieson, A. & Moenssens, A.A., eds.) 2009 [3] 1403.

4. FIBERS

T. W. Bierman, "Blocks of Colour IV: The Evidential Value of Blue and Red Cotton Fibres," 47 Science & Justice 68 (2006).

Caugh M. Bryant, "Palynology," in Wiley Encyclopedia of Forensic Science (Jamieson, A. & Moenssens, A.A., eds.) 2009 [4] 1954.

Kris De Wael, Fabrice G. Gason & Christiaan A. V. Baes, "Selection of an Adhesive Tape Suitable for Forensic Fiber Sampling," 53 J. Forensic Sciences 168 (2008).

L. Leon, K. De Wael, F. Gason & B. Gilbert, "Application of Raman Spectroscopy to Forensic Fibre Cases," 48 Science & Justice 109 (2008).

Menachem Lewin, *Handbook of Fiber Chemistry*, 3rd ed. 2007.

Kornelia Nehse, "Examination of Fibers and Textiles," in Wiley Encyclopedia of Forensic Science (Jamieson, A. & Moenssens, A.A., eds.) 2009 [2] 985.

Ray Palmer, William Hutchinson & Verity Fryer, "The Discrimination of (Non–Denim) Blue Cotton," 49 Science & Justice 12 (2009).

Claude Roux & James Robertson, "Fibers," in Wiley Encyclopedia of Forensic Science (Jamieson, A. & Moenssens, A.A., eds.) 2009 [3] 1095.

5. PAINT, GLASS, AND OTHER PHYSICAL EVIDENCE

David Baldwin, "Footwear and Foot Impressions: Intelligence," in Wiley Encyclopedia of Forensic Science (Jamieson, A. & Moenssens, A.A., eds.) 2009 [3] 1248.

David Baldwin, "Footwear and Foot Impressions: Databases," in Wiley Encyclopedia of Forensic Science (Jamieson, A. & Moenssens, A.A., eds.) 2009 [3] 1240.

William J. Bodziak, *"Tire Tread and Tire Track Evidence,"* 2008.

Vaughn M. Bryant, "Palynology," in Wiley Encyclopedia of Forensic Science (Jamieson, A. & Moenssens, A.A., eds.) 2009 [4] 1954.

Gareth P. Campbell & James M. Curran, "The Interpretation of Elemental Composition Measurements from Forensic Glass Evidence III," 49 SCIENCE & JUSTICE 2 (2009).

Anthony M. Cowell, "Wood," in WILEY ENCYCLOPEDIA OF FORENSIC SCIENCE (Jamieson, A. & Moenssens, A.A., eds.) 2009 [5] 2640.

James M. Curran & Tacha M. Hicks, "Glass Evidence: Bayesian Approach to," in WILEY ENCYCLOPEDIA OF FORENSIC SCIENCE (Jamieson, A. & Moenssens, A.A., eds.) 2009 [3] 1351.

Charl Du Presz & Claude Roux, "Tire Impressions," in WILEY ENCYCLOPEDIA OF FORENSIC SCIENCE (Jamieson, A. & Moenssens, A.A., eds.) 2009 [5] 2480.

N. L. Farmer, A. Ruffell, W. Meuier–Augenstein, J. Meneely & R. M. Kalin, "Forensic Analysis of Wooden Safety Matches," 47 SCIENCE AND JUSTICE 88 (2007).

Robert W. Fitzpatrick, "Soil: Forensic Analysis," in WILEY ENCYCLOPEDIA OF FORENSIC SCIENCE (Jamieson, A. & Moenssens, A.A., eds.) 2009 [5] 2377.

Leslie Hammer, "Footwear and Foot Impressions: Overview," in WILEY ENCYCLOPEDIA OF FORENSIC SCIENCE (Jamieson, A. & Moenssens, A.A., eds.) 2009 [3] 1252.

Leslie Hammer & Robert Kennedy, "Footwear and Foot Impressions: Foot Impressions and Linking Foot to Shoe," in WILEY ENCYCLOPEDIA OF FORENSIC SCIENCE (Jamieson, A. & Moenssens, A.A., eds.) 2009 [3] 1244.

James S. Hamiel & John S. Yoshida, "Evaluation and Application of Polynomial Texture Mapping in the Area of Shoe and Impression Evidence," 57 J. FORENSIC IDENTIFICATION 414 (2007).

Isaac Kereweer, "Footwear and Foot Impressions: Comparison and Identification," in WILEY ENCYCLOPEDIA OF FORENSIC SCIENCE (Jamieson, A. & Moenssens, A.A., eds.) 2009 [3] 1230.

Tina J. Lovelock, "Glass," in WILEY ENCYCLOPEDIA OF FORENSIC SCIENCE (Jamieson, A. & Moenssens, A.A., eds.) 2009 [3] 1348.

Susan Luong & Claude Roux, "Marks of Impressions of Manufactured Items," in WILEY ENCYCLOPEDIA OF FORENSIC SCIENCE (Jamieson, A. & Moenssens, A.A., eds.) 2009 [4] 1668.

Genevieve Massonet & Florence Monnard, "Paint: Interpretation," in WILEY ENCYCLOPEDIA OF FORENSIC SCIENCE (Jamieson, A. & Moenssens. A.A., eds.) 2009 [4] 1943.

John McCullough, "Paint," in WILEY ENCYCLOPEDIA OF FORENSIC SCIENCE (Jamieson, A. & Moenssens, A.A., eds.) 2009 [4] 1931.

Sean McDermott, "Trace Evidence: Transfer and Persistence," in WILEY ENCYCLOPEDIA OF FORENSIC SCIENCE (Jamieson, A. & Moenssens, A.A., eds.) 2009 [5] 2534.

Sara C. McNorton, Guy W. Nutter & Jay A. Siegel, "The Characterization of Automobile Body Fillers," 53 J. FORENSIC SCIENCES 116 (2008).

Lynn Meijerman, et al., "Inter–and Intra–Individual Variation in Applied Force when Listening at a Surface and Resulting Variation in Earprints," 46 MED. SCI. LAW [2] 141 (2006).

Lynn Meijerman, A. Thean & G. J. R. Maat, "Earprints: Interpretation of," in WILEY ENCYCLOPEDIA OF FORENSIC SCIENCE (Jamieson, A. & Moenssens, A.A., eds.) 2009 [2] 891.

N. S. Parsons & C. A. Mountain, "Investigating Polyurethane Foam as a Form of Trace Evidence," 48 SCIENCE & JUSTICE 24 (2007).

Kenneth Pye, *Geological and Soil Evidence*, 2007.

Roger M. Rowell, ed., *Handbook of Wood Chemistry and Wood Composites*, 2005.

William Schneck, "Particle: Form," in WILEY ENCYCLOPEDIA OF FORENSIC SCIENCE (Jamieson, A. & Moenssens, A.A., eds.) 2009 [4] 2001.

Eric Stauffer, "Light Bulbs and Filaments: Examination of," in WILEY ENCYCLOPEDIA OF FORENSIC SCIENCE (Jamieson, A. & Moenssens, A.A., eds.) 2009 [3] 1632.

Marc Tibbett & David O. Carter, eds., *"Soil Analysis in Forensic Pathonomy,"* 2008.

Kevan A. J. Walsh & Mark Horrocks, "Palynology: Its Position in the Field of Forensic Science," 53 J. FORENSIC SCIENCES 1053 (2008).

Chapter 12

SPECTROGRAPHIC VOICE RECOGNITION

————

II. THE SPECTROGRAPHIC VOICE RECOGNITION SYSTEM

§ 12.04   Theory of Voice Uniqueness

Page 795.   At the end of the section, *add the following additional paragraph*:

The difficulties encountered when attempting to separate the voices of twins from each other stem, according to prevailing theories, from the recognition that the development of the mechanism of speech is influenced not only by genetic influences, but also by environmental factors and behavior patterns. Thus, it is expected that if one twin smokes and the other does not, this would have an effect on the recognition of each twin's voice patterns. Similarly, physical separation at a fairly early age might result in dialectal differences that may manifest themselves subsequently in their voice development.

One carefully constructed biometric study conducted recently in London, U.K., sought to compare voices of 49 monozygotic twin pairs in research that focused particularly on the non-genetic factors, concluded tentatively that where twins experience independence, their voices may show dissimilarities that it is possible to exploit. This would tend to increase dramatically the discrimination capability of computer-assisted speaker verification. It would also, incidentally, provide support for the voice uniqueness assumption.

Speech samples were obtained through the cooperation of a Centre for Twin Research and Genetic Epidemiology at a London hospital. The impressive results of the experiment showed that the Equal Error Rate (EER %) was reduced to around 0.5% even when test utterances were of a duration of no more than 5 seconds.[1]

————

III.   EVIDENCE OF VOICE COMPARISONS BY SPECTROGRAMS

1. [New] Aladdin Ariyaeeinia, Christopher Morrison, Amit Malegaonkar & Sue Black, "A Test of the Effectiveness of Speaker Verification for Differentiating Between Identical Twins," 48 SCIENCE AND JUSTICE 182 (2008).

§ 12.09   Computer Assisted Voice Identification and Biometrics

Page 813.   At the end of the 3rd full paragraph, *insert the following additional sentences*:

While considerable progress has been made in automated comparisons, in the end human speech experts may be more adept at matching voice patterns than a computer can be. One prominent European researcher, in his research on a computer-assisted matching system, recently concluded:

> Expert-based methods are claimed to be more flexible for cases with qualitative and quantitative limitations and more robust for speech samples with strongly mismatched behavioral and technical conditions, or those containing linguistic or dialectal particularities. Finally, since experts are phoneticians or linguists, the expert-based methods are more easily explained in a court of justice, where they often perceive automatic methods as "black boxes."[2]

IV.   MISCELLANEOUS

§ 12.10   Bibliography of Additional References

Page 814.   *Insert the following entries*:

Aladdin Ariyaeeinia, J. Fortuna, P. Sivakumaran & A. Malegaonkar, "Verification Effectiveness in Open-set Speaker Identification," IEE Proceedings, Vision Image and Signal Processing 153 (5) (Oct. 2006) 618.

Aladdin Ariyaeeinia, Christopher Morrison, Amit Malegaonkar & Sue Black, "A Test of the Effectiveness of Speaker Verification for Differentiating Between Identical Twins," 48 Science and Justice 182 (2008).

N. Brummer & J. Du Prez, "Application–Independent Evaluation of Speaker Detection," 20 Computer Speech and Language 230 (2006).

J. Fortuna, A. Ariyaeeinia & A. Malegaonkar, "Open-set Speaker Identification, Using Adapted Gaussian Mixture Models," Proceedings 9th International Conf. On Speech Communication and Technology, Lisbon, Portugal, Sep. 2005, p. 1997.

J. Gonzales & A. Carpi, "Early Effects of Smoking on the Voice: A Multi–Dimensional Study," Medical Science Monitor, 10 (2004) CR649–CR656.

----

2. [New] Didier Meuwly, "Speaker Recognition," in Wiley Encyclopedia of Forensic Science (Jamieson, A. & Moenssens, A.A., eds.) 2009 [5] 2389 at 2392. The author further suggests a series of research proposals that may determine whether expert-based methods can be matched in efficiency with computer-assisted comparison systems, suggesting that much additional exploration is needed.

Didier Meuwly, "Speaker Recognition," in WILEY ENCYCLOPEDIA OF FORENSIC SCIENCE (Jamieson, A. & Moenssens, A.A., eds.) 2009 [5] 2389.

H. A. Patil & T. K. Basu, "Detection of Bilingual Twins by Teager Energy–Based Features," PROCEEDINGS OF THE INTERNATIONAL CONFERENCE ON SIGNAL PROCESSING AND COMMUNICATION, p. 32 (2004).

D. Ramos–Castro, *Forensic Evaluation of the Evidence Using Automatic Speaker Recognition Systems*, 2007.

D. Van Leuwen, A. Martin, M. Przybocki & J. Bouten, "NIST and NFI–TNO Evaluations of Automatic Speaker Recognition," 20 COMPUTER SPEECH AND LANGUAGE 128 (2006).

Chapter 13

FORENSIC ACCIDENT RECONSTRUCTION

I. INTRODUCTION

§ 13.01 Scope of the Chapter

Page 817, in footnote 2 *add*:

The Accident Reconstruction Communications Network also offers a wealth of information regarding reconstruction and traffic accident investigation. Its website address is http://www.accidentreconstruction.com; last viewed November 20, 2008.

II. THE INVESTIGATION OF ACCIDENTS

§ 13.07 Speed Estimation from Skidmarks and Yaw Marks

Page 822, paragraphs at the end of the section, *add the following*:

For an explanation of the effects of yaw rotation on vehicle deceleration see Mark Erickson & Wilson C. Hayes, *Drag Facto Attenuation for Rotating Vehicles*, 18 ACCIDENT RECONSTRUCTION J., May–June 2008, at 19.

Critical Speed Yaw (CSY) analysis is another technique reconstructionists use to determine a vehicle's speed. The investigator determines the speed by measuring the radius of the path of the turning vehicle and then analyzes the lateral acceleration to road friction. Wade Bartlett & William Wright, *Summary of 56 Recent Critical Speed Yaw Analysis Tests including ABS and Electronic Stability Control on Pavement, Gravel, and Grass*, 18 ACCIDENT RECONSTRUCTION J., May–June 2008, at 29.

For an illustration of a slide to stop analysis including pedestrian drag factor to determine a vehicle's speed see Michael Allison, *Cement Truck v. Pedestrian: A Case Study*, 18 ACCIDENT RECONSTRUCTION J., Mar.-Apr. 2008, at 41.

For a comparison of equations for estimating vehicle speed in frontal impacts with narrow objects such as poles and trees based upon maximum residual frontal crush see Joseph N. Colfone et al., *A Comparison of Equations for Estimating Speed Based on Maximum Static Deformation for Frontal Narrow–Object Impacts*, 17 ACCIDENT RECONSTRUCTION J., Nov.-Dec. 2007, at 19. Eight equations were tested including NTSB, Morgan and Ivey, Nystrom and Kost, The Craig Equations (Craig Crush

Depth = Sp. and Craig Modified), The Vomhof CF Method, Wood, and the Bilinear Equation.

Accident reconstructionists have also measured a vehicle's speed using information derived from a video tape that was positioned inside an officer's vehicle. For an explanation of this technique see Mark Kimsey, *Speed Calculation From a Video Tape*, 18 Accident Reconstruction J., July–Aug. 2008 at 23.

§ 13.08 Automobile "Black Boxes"

Page 822, *add to footnote 2*:

For a comprehensive compilation of technical research papers addressing EDRs see H. Clay Gabler et al., eds., Event Data Recorders: A Decade of Innovation, 2008. For information on EDRs in heavy vehicles (HV EDRs) see http://www.heavytruckedr.org, last viewed November 20, 2008.

Page 823. In footnote 3, *replace*:

http://dms.dot.gov with http://www.regulations.gov, last viewed November 20, 2008.

Page 825, *add to footnote 13*:

In 2003, Vetronix was acquired by ETAS, a supplier of standardized development and diagnostic tools for electronic control units and in 2006, the Vetronix Aftermarket division merged with Bosch Automotive Aftermarket, responsible for supply, sales and logistics of automotive parts for service of the vehicle. The respective website addresses are http://www.etas.com and http://www.boschdiagnostics.com, both last viewed November 20, 2008.

Page 825, in footnote 17, *replace (http://dms.dot.gov) in footnote 17 with*:

49 C.F.R. pt. 563 (2008) can be accessed at http://ecfr.gpoaccess.gov/cgi/t/text/text-idx?c=ecfr & tpl=/ecfrbrowse/Title49/49cfr563_main_02.tpl, last viewed November 20, 2008 or is available in Event Data Recorders supra note 2 at 413.

Page 825, *add to footnote 22*:

On November 20, 2006 George R. Weller was sentenced to five years of felony probation and ordered to pay about $90,000 in penalties, fines, and restitution. *No Jail For Elderly Driver in Market Crash*, CBS News, November 20, 2006, available at http://www.cbsnews.com/stories/2006/11/20/national/main2200813.shtml (last viewed November 20, 2008). The city of Santa Monica, its insurers, market operator Bayside District Corporation and George Weller entered into settlement agreements with parties who lost family members in the July 16, 2003 incident. Other plaintiffs had previously settled for $15.3 million. See Richard Winton & Martha Groves, *Case is Closed on Deadly Day at Market*, L.A.Times, May 22, 2008 at A1.

Page 826, *add to footnote 28*:

The list of vehicles equipped with EDR devices and the list of EDR state statutes were both updated on November 20, 2008. This information can be accessed at http://www.harristechnical.com/cdr.htm, last viewed November 20, 2008.

Page 827, at the end of § 13.08, *add the following text*:

Twelve states, including Arkansas, California, Colorado, Connecticut, Maine, New Hampshire, New York, Nevada, North Dakota, Oregon,

Texas, and Virginia now have statutes addressing EDR devices.[a] All of the statutes require vehicle owner consent to retrieve any data, barring a few exceptions. Consent is not required if the data is used solely for research purposes and identifying information is not disclosed. Another exception to consent arises in criminal cases when a search warrant is issued. The statutes vary with respect to how consent should be obtained.

All states, including those with EDR statutes, also have computer trespass statutes that may apply to EDR devices. The statutes mandate criminal penalties for invading or accessing computer information without the owner's consent. An EDR device may fit within the statutes' definitions of a computer.

EDR devices also raise several constitutional concerns. For detailed analyses of the constitutional implications of EDRs see generally: John Buhrman, *Riding with Little Brother: Striking a Better Balance Between the Benefits of Automobile Event Data Recorders and their Drawbacks*, 17 CORNELL J.L. & PUB. POL'Y 201 (2007); Andrew Askland, *The Double Edged Sword that is the Event Data Recorder*, 25 TEMP. J. SCI. TECH. & ENVTL. L. 1 (2006); and Kevin J. Powers, *David Hasselhoff No Longer Owns the Only Talking Car: Automotive Black Boxes in Criminal Law*, 39 SUFFOLK U.L. REV. 289 (2005).

A new type of EDR device is generating some additional concerns. Whereas EDR devices are only activated when a sensor is triggered, usually due to a vehicle crash, a Vehicle Status Data Recorder (VSDR) is constantly activated while recording information such as wheel and engine speed. It stores information for several days and cannot be deactivated. Vehicle manufacturers, such as Nissan, claim the device is an effective tool that mechanics can use to determine problems with the vehicle. In addition to privacy concerns, consumers may be troubled about its use in relation to warranty repairs. Nissan claims the information will not be used to invalidate warranties but would be used as a method to verify whether a vehicle had been abused or raced.[b]

In April 2008, the NHTSA released a report titled, *Analysis of Event Data Recorder Data for Vehicle Safety Improvement*.[c] NHTSA worked in collaboration with The Volpe Center to determine the reliability of EDR data in relation to crash reconstruction and improvement of vehicle safety systems. NHTSA supplied the Volpe Center with over 2,500 EDR files that had been downloaded from various systems. The main objective was to determine whether researchers should use EDR data to develop future safety features.

a. For a more detailed analysis of the state statutes see Jim Harris, *Event Data Recorders—State Statutes and Legal Consideration*, 18 ACCIDENT RECONSTRUCTION J., Jan.-Feb. 2008 at 50.

b. Bob Gritzinger, *Black Box on Board: New Standards for Automotive Big Brother Take Effect in 2012*, 10 ACCIDENT RECONSTRUCTION NEWSL., Sep. 2008, available at http://www.accidentreconstruction.com/newsletter/sep08/index.html, last viewed November 20, 2008.

c. The report can be accessed at http://www.nhtsa.dot.gov/staticfiles/DOT/NHTSA/NRD/Multimedia/PDFs/EDR/Research/810935.pdf, last viewed November 20, 2008.

As EDR devices become more advanced, reconstructionists are utilizing the data in various ways. A vehicle's change in velocity, designated by delta-V, is utilized to signify crash severity. Delta–V is normally estimated from computer codes such as WinSmash and Crash3. In many cases it is very difficult to estimate. Therefore, some reconstructionists are utilizing EDR data to establish delta-V.[d] EDR data has also been used to compare the ability of delta-V and the occupant impact velocity (OIV) to predict occupant injury in crashes.[e]

III. LEGAL STATUS OF ACCIDENT RECONSTRUCTION

§ 13.09 Admissibility of Accident Reconstruction Evidence

Page 827, insert *additional footnote (1a)* after the first sentence of the first paragraph:

1a. In North Carolina, expert witnesses were not permitted to testify regarding the speed at which a vehicle was traveling unless he or she observed the accident. *Shaw v. Sylvester*, 253 N.C. 176, 116 S.E.2d 351 (1960) (holding that a person who does not witness a vehicle's movement is not allowed to opine about its speed). The North Carolina legislature overruled *Shaw* when it amended Rule 702. The amended rule N.C. Gen. Stat § 8C–1, Rule 702(i) states: "A witness qualified as an expert in accident reconstruction who has performed a reconstruction of a crash, or has reviewed the report of investigation, with proper foundation may give an opinion as to the speed of a vehicle even if the witness did not observe the vehicle moving." The effective date of the amendment is December 1, 2006. The statute can be accessed at http://www.ncga.state.nc.us/EnactedLegislation/Statutes/HTML/ByChapter/Chapter_8C.html, last viewed November 20, 2008.

Page 827, after first sentence of second paragraph, *add additional footnote (1b)*:

1b. In *Dahlgren v. Muldrow*, 2008 WL 186641 (N.D.Fla.2008) the plaintiff sought to exclude lay opinion testimony regarding whether the defendant had a legal duty to stop at an inoperative traffic sign. The court reaffirmed the general rule that lay and expert witnesses cannot testify about questions of law but denied plaintiff's motion because he did not name which witness or indicate which statement he sought to exclude.

Page 827, *add to footnote 3*:

For information on non-eyewitness testimony regarding a vehicle's speed see generally "Expert or opinion testimony as to speed of vehicle by one who had no view, or only

d. See Hampton C. Gabler et al., *Estimating Crash Severity: Can Event Data Recorders Replace Crash Reconstruction?* 10 ACCIDENT RECONSTRUCTION NEWSL., April 2008, available at http://accidentreconstruction.com/newsletter/apr08/index.html, last viewed November 20, 2008. For an analysis of the ability of EDRs to accurately capture delta-V see Peter Niehoff et al., *Evaluation of Event Data Recorders in Full Systems Crash Tests*, 8 ACCIDENT RECONSTRUCTION NEWSL., Dec. 2006, available at http://www.accidentreconstruction.com/newsletter/dec06.asp#EDR, last viewed November 20, 2008.

e. See D. J. Gabauer & H. C. Gabler, *Comparison of Delta–V and Occupant Impact Velocity Crash Severity Metrics Using Event Data Recorders*, 9 ACCIDENT RECONSTRUCTION NEWSL., Mar. 2007, available at http://www.accidentreconstruction.com/newsletter/mar07.asp#EDR, last viewed November 20, 2008.

momentary view, of vehicle at time of accident" 156 A.L.R. 382 (2008).

Page 828, *add to footnote 5*:

Compare to *Fisher v. Central Cab Co.*, 945 A.2d 215 (Pa.Super.2008). Appellants argued that the trial court erred in allowing a lay witness to testify about the speed of appellant's vehicle. The court disagreed. The lay witness was a passenger on the bus that the appellant's vehicle hit. The witness was sitting in the front row of the bus and was easily able to observe appellant's vehicle 50 to 100 feet before the accident. The court held that the testimony satisfied the *Radogna* requirements for admissibility of lay witness speed estimations.

Page 830, *add to footnote 15*:

But see *Bermudez v. Capital Area Transp. Auth.*, 2007 WL 4553626 (Mich.App.2007) (affirming denial of summary judgment motion because the expert based his testimony on conflicting eyewitness reports).

Page 831, *add to footnote 20*:

Compare to *Moreno v. W.R. Davis Produce, Inc.*, 2007 WL 1731139 (W.D.Tex.2007) (granting plaintiff's motion to exclude testimony from a state trooper regarding which vehicle crossed the center line).

Page 831, *add to footnote 21*:

Compare to *People v. Sabapathy*, 2007 WL 4179321 (Mich.App.2007) (unpublished). The appellate court held that the trial court erred in violating Mich. R. Evid. 703 by allowing the accident reconstructionist to testify about the speed of the vehicle based on hearsay statements from witnesses. Although the court held that this was error, it was not reversible error due to other evidence present at trial.

Page 833, *add to footnote 25*:

Compare to *Bowman v. Pennington*, 2007 WL 437782 (D.Kan.2007). The court granted defendant's request to exclude sections of the investigating officer's report that addressed the cause and contributing factors of the accident. The court stated this was for the jury to determine because it went to the ultimate issue of who was legally responsible for the accident.

Page 835, *add to footnote 34*:

See *State v. Shabazz*, 400 N.J.Super. 203, 946 A.2d 626 (2005) (concluding that the *Frye* standards were satisfied because event data recorder evidence is reliable and generally accepted within the automotive and accident reconstruction community).

Page 836, at the end of this section, *add the following*:

In *Librado v. M.S. Carriers*,[a] the U.S. District Court for the Northern District of Texas held that an accident reconstructionist's testimony based on information obtained from a black box was reliable and admissible under the *Daubert* standard.

In *Commonwealth v. Zimmermann*,[b] the defendant was driving a 2002 GMC Yukon sport utility vehicle during a rain/snow storm. She lost control of the vehicle and struck a tree on the passenger's side. The passenger died. The driver was charged and convicted of motor vehicle

---

a. 2004 WL 1335942 (N.D.Tex.2004).

b. 70 Mass.App.Ct. 357, 873 N.E.2d 1215 (2007).

homicide by negligent operation. At trial, the Commonwealth sought to admit evidence regarding the driver's rate of speed five seconds before the incident. This information had been obtained from the vehicle's EDR. The trial judge held that the Commonwealth's expert was qualified as an expert and the EDR was an accurate device. Under the *Lanagin/Daubert* standard, the judge determined that there was general acceptance in the scientific community of the validity of such data. The appellate court held that this was not an abuse of discretion and affirmed the trial court's rulings.

§ 13.10   Qualifications of the Reconstruction Expert

Page 837, in § 13.10—Qualifications of the Accident Reconstruction Expert, *add the following to the list of associations*:

- Accident Reconstruction Communication Network
- American Society for Materials
- American Society of Biomechanics (ASB)
- American Society of Mechanical Engineers (ASME)
- Australasian and South Pacific Association of Collision Investigators (ASPACI)
- California Association of Accident Reconstruction Specialists (CAARS)
- Colorado State Patrol (CSP)
- Denver Research Institute (DRI)-University of Denver
- European Association for Accident Research and Analysis
- Forensic Accident Reconstructionists of Oregon (FARO)
- Illinois Association of Technical Accident Investigators (IATAI)
- Indiana Association of Certified Accident Investigators (IACAI)
- Institute of Traffic Accident Investigators (United Kingdom)
- Maryland Association of Traffic Accident Investigators (MdATAI)
- Michigan Association of Traffic Accident Investigators (MATAI)
- Michigan State Police (MSP)
- Midwest Association of Technical Accident Investigators (MwATAI)
- National Society of Professional Engineers (NSPE)
- New Jersey Association of Accident Reconstructionists (NJAAR)
- New York Statewide Traffic Accident Reconstruction Society (NYSTARS)
- Ontario Provincial Police (OPP)
- Oregon State Police (OSP)
- Pennsylvania State Police (PSP)
- Professional Society of Forensic Mapping (PSFM)

- Registered Professional Engineers
- Southeastern Accident Reconstructions Society (SARS)
- Southwestern Association of Technical Accident Investigators (SA-TAI)
- Texas Association of Accident Reconstruction Specialists (TAARS)
- University of Central Missouri (UCMO)
- Washington Association of Technical Accident Investigators (WA-TAI)

Page 837, *replace the third sentence of the second paragraph with*:

ACTAR has approximately 700 accredited reconstructionists practicing throughout the United States, Canada, Australia, Singapore and the United Arab Emirates.

Page 838, after the paragraph that discusses *Mathieu v. Schnitzer,* **add the following**:

In *Favia v. Ford Motor Co.*,[c] the appellate court held that the trial court did not abuse discretion in permitting two officers to testify as experts. One of the officers had worked in law enforcement since 1991 and had studied accident investigation at the Indiana Law Enforcement Academy, with additional training in accident investigation. The officer estimated that he had investigated approximately 75 crashes annually, including several rollovers. The second officer began his law enforcement career as a road deputy in 1976 and had attended 80 hours of crash investigation school and 40 hours of advanced technical crash investigation.

The court ruled "it was not fanciful, arbitrary or unreasonable for the trial court to allow the police to give causation testimony, based on their years of experience and real-world expertise as accident investigators."[d] The court also noted that "their lack of particular scientific or academic knowledge goes to the weight of their testimony, not its admissibility."[e]

Page 838, *add to footnote 4*:

See also *State v. DeWalt*, 2007 WL 2851930 (Ohio App.2007) (holding that the trial court abused its discretion by allowing an officer to testify as an expert reconstructionist when he was only qualified as an expert accident investigator).

Page 839, *add to footnote 5*:

Compare to *Vigil v. Michelin*, 2007 WL 2778233 (W.D.Tex.2007). The court addressed the qualifications of two potential expert witnesses. Regarding the first witness, the court held that he was qualified as an expert despite only having one semester of education after high school. He had four-teen years of police department experience, several years of which were focused on investigating major traffic accidents plus additional training on different investigative methods. He also had eighteen years of experience in private traffic accident recon-

c. 381 Ill.App.3d 809, 320 Ill.Dec. 113, 886 N.E.2d 1182 (2008).

d. *Id.* at 1190.

e. *Id.*

struction and commercial investigations. Regarding the second witness, the court held that due to his training and experience he was qualified as an expert to testify about the cause of the accident, the vehicle's speed, the appearance of the tires at the scene, and any other observations or measurements derived from the scene. However, the court ruled that the second witness was not qualified as a tire expert and could not testify about what caused the tires to split.

Page 839, after the paragraph that discusses *Bales v. Shelton*, add the following:

The Georgia Appellate Court followed this reasoning in *Fortner v. Town of Register*.[d] The Court affirmed the trial court's ruling permitting two expert witnesses to testify. The appellant argued that it was error to allow the investigating officer to opine that a contributing factor in the case was that the decedent truck driver had failed to stop at the railroad stop sign. The Court held that it was not error to admit this testimony because the officer was qualified as an expert and his opinion was based on his examination of the accident scene and eyewitness testimony.[e]

The appellant also argued that it was error to allow a truck driver to give an expert opinion about whether a truck driver could have seen a train coming at the railroad crossing. Although the appellant did not properly preserve the objection for appeal, even if it had been properly preserved, the Court ruled that the testimony would have been admissible. The expert witness had thirty years of experience as a truck driver and had sixteen years of experience teaching truck drivers. Due to his truck driving experience, which included maneuvering at railroad crossings, his testimony was admissible. However, the court restricted his testimony to whether a truck driver could have seen the train coming at the crossing.[f]

Page 842, *add to footnote 14*:

Compare to *Morris v. Florida Transformer, Inc.*, 455 F.Supp.2d 1328, 1332–1333 (M.D.Ala.2006) (holding that plaintiff's expert in accident reconstruction was not qualified to give an expert opinion as to the cause of death).

§ 13.11   Bases of Expert Opinion

Page 843, *add to footnote 2*:

Compare to *Powell v. W & W Hauling, Inc.*, 226 Fed.Appx. 950, 954 (11th Cir.2007) (affirming trial court's decision permitting the defendant's expert to base his opinion on evidence previously presented by the defendant regarding the degree of intoxication of plaintiff's son).

§ 13.12   Use of Demonstrative Evidence

Page 847, *add to footnote 5*:

Compare to *Hammond v. Salvation Army*, 2006 WL 2271309 (Mich.App.2006) (holding

---

d. 289 Ga.App. 543, 657 S.E.2d 620 (2008).

e. Id.

f. See also *Donihe v. Young*, 2006 WL 5249717 (N.D.Ga.2006). The court permitted a dump truck driver to testify as an expert witness regarding whether a dump truck driver should have known that a rock was stuck in the truck's tires. The court held that because the witness had been a dump truck driver since he was eighteen he had more knowledge on the subject than an average juror and therefore he was qualified as an expert.

that the trial court abused its discretion in admitting a videotape produced by the defendant's expert because the videotape was not relevant to a contested issue in the case).

§ 13.13   Sufficiency of Evidence and Other Legal Issues

Page 853, at the end of the section, *add the following*:

In criminal cases, courts have held that the failure to obtain an expert in accident reconstruction resulted in ineffective assistance of counsel. In *State v. Olson*,[a] Olson was convicted of homicide by intoxicated use of a motor vehicle. The evidence showed that Olson's vehicle crossed the center line and struck another vehicle, killing the driver. At trial, Olson argued that the accident was caused due to the road conditions and not because he was intoxicated. Olson's attorney did not call any witnesses other than Olson himself, did not retain an expert or seek an adjournment to hire an expert, did not investigate the scene of the accident, did not obtain weather reports on the date of the accident, and did not obtain information about other accidents that occurred in the county on the same day.

Olson filed a postconviction motion for a new trial based on ineffective assistance of counsel. At the postconviction hearing, an expert accident reconstructionist's testimony corroborated Olson's theory but the trial court denied the motion. On appeal, the Wisconsin Court of Appeals concluded that Olson's attorney had rendered ineffective assistance of counsel by not seeking an adjournment of trial and retaining an accident reconstruction expert. Finding this deficiency to be prejudicial, the Court reversed the conviction and remanded for a new trial.

In *Strandlien v. State*,[b] Strandlien was convicted of aggravated vehicular homicide. Strandlien appealed on various grounds including ineffective assistance of counsel. He argued that his attorney failed to hire an expert in accident reconstruction and therefore he was denied effective assistance of counsel, which he claimed was prejudicial to his case. The Supreme Court of Wyoming agreed because the nature of the collision was a main issue in the case and it was necessary to retain an expert accident reconstructionist to provide adequate assistance of counsel. The Court reversed the conviction and remanded the case.

In contrast, in *Deskins v. Zenon*,[c] the United States District Court for the District of Colorado dismissed defendant's ineffective assistance of counsel claim. Defendant had been convicted on various charges including vehicular homicide. For strategic reasons, the defendant's attorney did not hire an expert in accident reconstruction. The Court held that the defendant did not meet his burden of overcoming the presumption that his attorney had met the requisite level of assistance. Additionally, the court denied his claim because he failed to specifically show how an expert witness would have helped his case.

---

a. 296 Wis.2d 934, 724 N.W.2d 273 (App.2006) (unpublished).

b. 156 P.3d 986 (Wyo.2007).

c. 2007 WL 1701717 (D.Colo.2007).

IV. MISCELLANEOUS

§ 13.14   Bibliography of Selected References

Page 853. Correct the section number from § 11.14 to § 13.14:

1. JOURNALS

Page 853. *Add this entry:*

COLLISION MAGAZINE: THE INTERNATIONAL COMPENDIUM FOR CRASH RESEARCH, Collision Publishing, LLC.

2. BOOKS AND ARTICLES

Page 853. *Add the following entries:*

Michael Allison, "Cement Truck v. Pedestrian: A Case Study," 18 ACCIDENT RECONSTRUCTION J., Mar.-Apr. 2008.

Andrew Askland, "The Double Edged Sword that is the Event Data Recorder," 25 TEMP. J. SCI. TECH. & ENVTL. L. 1 (2006).

Wade Bartlett & William Wright, "Summary of 56 Recent Critical Speed Yaw Analysis Tests Including ABS and Electronic Stability Control on Pavement, Gravel, and Grass," 18 ACCIDENT RECONSTRUCTION J., May–June 2008.

John Buhrman, *"Riding with Little Brother: Striking a Better Balance Between the Benefits of Automobile Event Data Recorders and their Drawbacks,"* 17 CORNELL J.L. & PUB. POL'Y 201 (2007).

Joseph N. Colfone et al., "A Comparison of Equations for Estimating Speed Based on Maximum Static Deformation for Frontal Narrow–Object Impacts," 17 ACCIDENT RECONSTRUCTION J., Nov.-Dec. 2007.

Mark Erickson & Wilson C. Hayes, *Drag Facto Attenuation for Rotating Vehicles*, 18 ACCIDENT RECONSTRUCTION J., May–June 2008.

Expert or Opinion Testimony as to Speed of Vehicle by One Who Had No View, or Only Momentary View, of Vehicle at Time of Accident, 156 A.L.R. 382 (2008).

D. J. Gabauer & H. C. Gabler, "Comparison of Delta–V and Occupant Impact Velocity Crash Severity Metrics Using Event Data Recorders," 9 ACCIDENT RECONSTRUCTION NEWSL., Mar. 2007.

H. Clay Gabler et al., eds., EVENT DATA RECORDERS: A DECADE OF INNOVATION, 2008.

Hampton C. Gabler, et al., *"Estimating Crash Severity: Can Event Data Recorders Replace Crash Reconstruction?"* 10 ACCIDENT RECONSTRUCTION NEWSL. April 2008.

Bob Gritzinger, "Black Box on Board: New Standards for Automotive Big Brother Take Effect in 2012," 10 ACCIDENT RECONSTRUCTION NEWSL., Sep. 2008.

Jim Harris, "*Event Data Recorders—State Statutes and Legal Consideration*," 18 ACCIDENT RECONSTRUCTION J., Jan.-Feb. 2008.

Mark Kimsey, "Speed Calculation From a Video Tape," 18 ACCIDENT RECONSTRUCTION J., July–Aug. 2008 at 23.

Kevin J. Powers, "David Hasselhoff No Longer Owns the Only Talking Car: Automotive Black Boxes in Criminal Law," 39 SUFFOLK U.L. REV. 289 (2005).

Peter Niehoff et al., "Evaluation of Event Data Recorders in Full Systems Crash Tests", 8 ACCIDENT RECONSTRUCTION NEWSL., Dec. 2006.

*

Part III

EXPERT TESTIMONY IN THE BIOLOGICAL AND LIFE SCIENCES

Chapter 14

FORENSIC PATHOLOGY

I. INTRODUCTION

§ 14.03   Coroner System

Page 869. At the end of the section, *insert the following new subheading*:

THE 2009 NATIONAL ACADEMY OF SCIENCE (NAS) REPORT ON STRENGTHENING THE FORENSIC SCIENCES IN THE UNITED STATES

An announced elsewhere,[1] the National Academy of Science Report[2] made significant remarks about a number of forensic disciplines. It singled out the medical examination of death for separate whole-chapter treatment. The report's Chapter 9 is titled, "Medical Examiners and Coroner Systems: Current and Future Needs."[3]

Tracing the history of the coroner system from its beginnings in the tenth century, the method of legal death investigation was subsequently also imported, along with the adoption of British common Law, in the United States. While, over the years, some states or localities began to require that medical investigations be conducted by physicians or persons with medical training, and some jurisdictions did in fact institute medical examiner systems, it was not until the mid–1920s that serious criticism began to be leveled against elected coroner systems.[4] Recommendations were made to abolish the coroner system as an anachronistic institution that was incapable of determining competently the medical as well as the legal causes of a suspicious death. The suggestion to abolish

---

1. See, supra, page 4 of this Supplement. The NAS Report also has been discussed in connection with its impact on several other forensic disciplines. See, e.g., supplementary materials in Chapters 7, 8, 9, 10, and 11.

2. Hereafter referred to as either "the report," or the 2009 NAS Report.

3. NAS Report at 9–1.

4. The historical development of the origin, growth, and gradual decline in its acceptance as a workable system of death investigation is discussed both in the report, and at pp. 867 *et seq.* of the main text.

the coroner system was always accompanied by the recommendation that all states adopt a medical examiner system.[5]

With that background and a series of unfortunate events resulting from coroner-based examinations into the cause and manner of death, it is not a surprise that, after a lengthy exploration of the state of both medical examiner and coroner systems in America,[6] the National Academy of Science joined the chorus, when it ended its Chapter 9 with the following recommendation, quoted here in its entirety[7]:

Recommendation 11:

To improve medicolegal death investigation:

(a) Congress should authorize and appropriate incentive funds to the National Institute of Forensic Science (NIFS) for allocation to states and jurisdictions to establish medical examiner systems, with the goal of replacing and eventually eliminating existing coroner systems. Funds are needed to build regional medical examiner offices, secure necessary equipment, improve administration, and ensure the education, training, and staffing of medical examiner offices. Funding could also be used to help current medical examiner systems modernize their facilities to meet current Centers for Disease Control and Prevention—recommended autopsy safety requirements.

(b) Congress should appropriate resources to the National Institutes of Health (NIH) and NIFS, jointly, to support research, education, and training in forensic pathology. NIH, with NIFS participation, or NIFS in collaboration with content experts, should establish a study section to establish goals, to review and evaluate proposals in these areas, and to allocate funding for collaborative research to be conducted by medical examiner offices and medical universities. In addition, funding, in the form of medical student loan forgiveness and/or fellowship support, should be made available to pathology residents who choose forensic pathology as their specialty.

(c) NIFS, in collaboration with NIH, the National Association of Medical Examiners, the American Board of Medicolegal Death Investigators, and other appropriate professional organizations, should establish a Scientific Working Group (SWG) for forensic pathology and medicolegal death investigation. The SWG should develop and promote standards for best practices, administration, staffing, education, training, and continuing education for competent death scene investigations and postmortem examinations. Best practices should include the utilization of new tech-

---

5. For a discussion on the development in the United States of medical examiner systems in lieu of the existing antiquated coroner systems for the medical-legal investigation of death, see § 14.02, at pp. 863 et seq. of the main text.

6. 2009 NAS Report at pp. 9–1 through 9–20.

7. 2009 NAS Report, at pp. 9–20/21.

nologies such as laboratory testing for the molecular basis of diseases and the implementation of specialized imaging techniques.

(d) All medical examiner offices should be accredited pursuant to NIFS–endorsed standards within a timeframe to be established by NIFS.

(e) All federal funding should be restricted to accredited offices that meet NIFS–endorsed standards or that demonstrate significant and measurable progress in achieving accreditation within prescribed deadlines.

(f) All medicolegal autopsies should be performed or supervised by a board certified forensic pathologist. This requirement should take effect within a timeframe to be established by NIFS, following consultation with governing state institutions.

One would imagine that with this broad endorsement of what has been long a popular position of medical examiners and their accrediting bodies who sought to eliminate coroner systems, the NAS Report would merit enthusiastic support among medical examiners. Yet, an informal poll of some medical examiners shows a lot of skepticism that anything drastic or useful can come from it.

Coroner systems have a lot of adherents. There must be reasons why coroners represent the only governmental institution that has remained unchanged since colonial days. Perhaps the main reason is that the elected citizens of voting age eligible to become coroners need have no prior experience or medical education. They are also by far the majority. Almost half the counties in the U.S. are coroner counties. In New York alone, 50 of the 62 New York State counties are coroner counties, including its capital city of Albany, where the coroners are or have been insurance salesmen. (In most systems, the elected office of coroner is held by funeral directors!)

When attempts are made to have a state legislature pass a state medical examiner bill, the proposal is either dropped or defeated when the coroners—and the voters who elected them—show up in force at the legislature to oppose the bill.

Even among medical examiners who ought to wholeheartedly support cries for universal medical examiner agencies, there is some ambivalence. Some serious errors have occurred in determining causes of death at autopsy, as where pathologists ascribed a suspicious death as caused by blunt force trauma due to accident, and missed bullet wounds to the head (which would have made the death a homicide), or, conversely, finding a death due to criminal means and failing to discover fatal disease factors later determined to have been the cause of death.

Despite the professed scientific impartiality of medically-trained forensic pathologists, most exhibit a strong association with law enforcement and consider themselves "team players." They may fear the recommended strong "oversight" and insistence on the need for "best practices," continuing education, and quality control standards that they may be required to satisfy. No medical examiner has ever gotten into trouble for testifying in support of the prosecutor's theory, even when it turns that the defendant was innocent. Many do not want anyone checking the accuracy of their autopsies, yet many such examinations are poorly and cursorily performed. If is no surprise that the solve rate for murders has dropped from the 80% + in the 1970s to less than 50% currently, and has contributed to the conviction of innocents and the concomitant ability of the guilty to continue to commit crimes.

Though the state of medical-legal death investigation is in serious need of overhaul and the NAS recommendation is needed, an unknown percentage of medical examiners may hunker down for the status quo.

Not to be overlooked is the fact that abolishing the office of coroner would require a considerable change in state laws, not to mention those states where the position of coroner is an elected office provided for in state constitutions. There are serious political issues and alliances that come into play in any such attempt for radical change or abolition. All of these facts bode poorly for the major change in existing systems that the report recommends.

II. POSTMORTEM DETERMINATIONS

§ 14.06   Causes of Death

1.   ANOXIA (Asphyxia)

Page 881. At the end of footnote 10, *add the following*:

See also, Michael Pollanen, "Asphyxia," in Wiley Encyclopedia of Forensic Science (Jamieson, A. & Moenssens, A.A., eds.) 2009 [1] 224.

2.   WOUNDS

b.   Bullet Wounds

Page 897. At the end of the first paragraph in the subsection (line 9), *add a new footnote*:

33a. For an recent extensive discussion of the topic of bullet wounds, liberally illustrated by color photography, see Steve Pollak and Pekka J. Sauko, "Gunshot Wounds," in Wiley Encyclopedia of Forensic Science (Jamieson, A. & Moenssens, A.A., eds.) 2009 [3] 1380.

§ 14.07 The Forensic Pathologist in Civil Cases

2. TRAFFIC FATALITIES

Page 928. At the end of footnote 16, *add the following text*:

Also see, Anders F. Eriksson & Mars G. Ostrom, "Traffic Fatalities," in WILEY ENCY- CLOPEDIA OF FORENSIC SCIENCE (Jamieson, A. & Moenssens, A.A., eds.) 2009 [5] 2541.

3. MEDICAL MALPRACTICE

Page 931. At the end of the first paragraph in the subsection (line 7), *insert a new footnote*:

19. See, e.g., Drake v. Portuondo, 553 F.3d 230, a reversal of the denial of a writ of habeas corpus after a finding of guilt on two counts of murder, wherein an expert had testified regarding the fictional syndrome of sexual dysfunction, dubbed "picquerism," which the court characterized as "medically speaking, nonsense." The expert witness, retained by the prosecutor (but whose credentials were not investigated initially) testified falsely that he had been employed by the Los Angeles County Coroner's office, assisting in countless medico-legal investigations of death, when in fact he had been working there to clean and maintain the forensic lab. The expert witness was also found to have lied about other "qualifications." The facts of the case are mentioned, infra, in the text that accompanies footnote 20 on page 945.

See also, Burkhead Madea, "Medical Malpractice," in WILEY ENCYCLOPEDIA OF FORENSIC SCIENCE (Jamieson, A. & Moenssens, A.A., eds.) 2009 [4] 1689.

III. PATHOLOGICAL FINDINGS AS EVIDENCE

§ 14.10 Pathologist as an Expert Witness

Page 945. At the end of footnote 20, *add*:

But see also 553 F. 3d 230 for later developments in this case.

V. MISCELLANEOUS

§ 14.16 Bibliography of Additional References

Page 963. *Insert the following additional sources*:

Elizabeth Abraham, Margaret Cox & David Quincey, "Pigmentation: Postmortem Iris Color Change in the Eyes of *Sus scrofaI,*" 53 J. FORENSIC SCIENCE 626 (2008).

Anil Aggrawal, *Forensic and Medico–Legal Aspects of Sexual Crimes and Unusual Sexual Practices*, 2009.

William Bernet & Neelanjan Ray, "Child Sexual Abuse," in WILEY ENCYCLOPEDIA OF FORENSIC SCIENCE (Jamieson, A. & Moenssens, A.A., eds.) 2009 [2] 529.

Jochen Beyer, "Poisons: Detection of Naturally Occurring Poisons," in WILEY ENCYCLOPEDIA OF FORENSIC SCIENCE (Jamieson, A. & Moenssens, A.A., eds.) 2009 [4] 2057.

Sue Black & Lucina Hackman, "Disaster Victim Identification," in WILEY ENCYCLOPEDIA OF FORENSIC SCIENCE (Jamieson, A. & Moenssens, A.A., eds.) 2009 [2] 697.

Michael Bohnert, "Injury: Burns, Scalds, and Chemical," in WILEY ENCYCLOPEDIA OF FORENSIC SCIENCE (Jamieson, A. & Moenssens, A.A., eds.) 2009 [3] 1529.

Jason H. Byrd & James L. Castner, *Forensic Entomology* (2008).

Cristina Cattaneo, Davide Porta & Danilo De Angelis, "Identification of Human Remains," in WILEY ENCYCLOPEDIA OF FORENSIC SCIENCE (Jamieson, A. & Moenssens, A.A., eds.) 2009 [3] 1511.

Cristina Cattaneo & Davide Porta. "Trauma Analysis of Skeletal Remains," in WILEY ENCYCLOPEDIA OF FORENSIC SCIENCE (Jamieson, A. & Moenssens, A.A., eds.) 2009 [5] 2557.

Wing–Chi Cheng, "Postmortem Toxicology: Laboratory Analysis," in WILEY ENCYCLOPEDIA OF FORENSIC SCIENCE (Jamieson, A. & Moenssens, A.A., eds.) 2009 [4] 2119.

Melissa Connor, "Mass Grave Investigation," in WILEY ENCYCLOPEDIA OF FORENSIC SCIENCE (Jamieson, A. & Moenssens, A.A., eds.) 2009 [1] 224.

Mary Coulombe & Sxharon Johnson, "Southern Nevada Public Health Lab Gears Up for Bioterrorism: Forensic Magazine," Dec. 2006/Jan. 2007, p. 29.

Vincent J. M. DiMaio & Suzanna E. Dana, *Handbook of Forensic Pathology*, 2nd ed., 2007.

Olaf Drummer & Dimitri Gerostamoulos, "Postmortem Toxicology: Interpretation," in WILEY ENCYCLOPEDIA OF FORENSIC SCIENCE (Jamieson, A. & Moenssens, A.A., eds.) 2009 [4] 2115.

Anders F. Eriksson & Mats G. Ostrom, "Traffic Fatalities," M in WILEY ENCYCLOPEDIA OF FORENSIC SCIENCE (Jamieson, A. & Moenssens, A.A., eds.) 2009 [1] 224.

Scott I. Fairgrieve, *Forensic Cremation—Recovery and Analysis*, 2008.

Vittorio Fineschi & Emanuela Turillazzi, "Natural Causes of Sudden Death: Noncardiac," in WILEY ENCYCLOPEDIA OF FORENSIC SCIENCE (Jamieson, A. & Moenssens, A.A., eds.) 2009 [4] 1843.

D. E. Gennard, *Forensic Entomology: An Introduction*, 2007.

Robert P. Granacher, Jr., *Traumatic Brain Injury*, 2007.

Randy Hanzlick, *Death Investigation: Systems and Procedures*, 2007.

Perry Hookman, *Medical Malpractice Expert Witnessing*, 2007.

Steven B. Karch, Vittorio Fineschi & Irene Riezzo, "Cardiac and Natural Causes of Death," in WILEY ENCYCLOPEDIA OF FORENSIC SCIENCE (Jamieson, A. & Moenssens, A.A., eds.) 2009 [2] 468.

Jean Keeling & Anthony Busuttil, eds., *Paediatric Forensic Medicine and Pathology*, 2008.

Gerhard Kernbach–Wighton, "Postmortem Biochemical Examinations," in WILEY ENCYCLOPEDIA OF FORENSIC SCIENCE (Jamieson, A. & Moenssens, A.A., eds.) 2009 [4] 2076.

Jameds L. Knoll, IV & Michael M. Baden, "Autoerotic Deaths," in WILEY ENCYCLOPEDIA OF FORENSIC SCIENCE (Jamieson, A. & Moenssens, A.A., eds.) 2009 [1] 243.

Celia Kremer, Stephanie Racette, Charles–Antoine Dionne & Anny Sauvageau, "Discrimination of Falls and Blows in Blunt Head Trauma: Systematic Study of the Hat Brim Line Rule in Relation to Skull Fractures," 53 J. FORENSIC SCIENCES 716 (2008).

Marc A. Lebeau, "Drug–Facilitated Sexual Assault," in WILEY ENCYCLOPEDIA OF FORENSIC SCIENCE (Jamieson, A. & Moenssens, A.A., eds.) 2009 [2] 868.

Laura L. Liptai, "Trauma Causation: Analysis of Automotive," in WILEY ENCYCLOPEDIA OF FORENSIC SCIENCE (Jamieson, A. & Moenssens, A.A., eds.) 2009 [5] 2565.

Burkhard Madea, "Medical Malpractice,"in WILEY ENCYCLOPEDIA OF FORENSIC SCIENCE (Jamieson, A. & Moenssens, A.A., eds.) 2009 [4] 1689.

Burkhard Madea, "Death: Time of," in WILEY ENCYCLOPEDIA OF FORENSIC SCIENCE (Jamieson, A. & Moenssens, A.A., eds.) 2009 [2] 697.

Burkhard Madea, "Time of Death Determinations," in WILEY ENCYCLOPEDIA OF FORENSIC SCIENCE (Jamieson, A. & Moenssens, A.A., eds.) 2009 [5] 2466.

Richard W. Merritt & M. Eric Benbow, "Entomology," in WILEY ENCYCLOPEDIA OF FORENSIC SCIENCE (Jamieson, A. & Moenssens, A.A., eds.) 2009 [2] 935.

D. K. Molina, *Handbook of Forensic Toxicology for Medical Examiners*, 2009.

Gregory Murrey & Donald Starzinski, *The Forensic Evaluation of Traumatic Brain Injury*, 2007.

Bobbi Jo O'Neal, *Investigating Infant Deaths*, 2007.

Stefan Pollak & Pekka J. Sauko, "Gunshot Wounds," in WILEY ENCYCLOPEDIA OF FORENSIC SCIENCE (Jamieson, A. & Moenssens, A.A., eds.) 2009 [3] 1380.

Stefan Pollak & Pekka J. Sauko, "Wounds: Sharp Injury," in WILEY ENCYCLOPEDIA OF FORENSIC SCIENCE (Jamieson, A. & Moenssens, A.A., eds.) 2009 [5] 2646.

Michael Pollanen "Asphyxia," in WILEY ENCYCLOPEDIA OF FORENSIC SCIENCE (Jamieson, A. & Moenssens, A.A., eds.) 2009 [1] 224.

Patrick Randolph–Quinney, Xanthe Mallet & Sue Black, "Anthropology," in WILEY ENCYCLOPEDIA OF FORENSIC SCIENCE (Jamieson, A. & Moenssens, A.A., eds.) 2009 [1] 152.

James A. Romano, Brian J. Lukey & Harry Salem, eds., *Chemical Warfare Agents*, 2007.

Basil M. RuDusky, *Forensic Cardiovascular Medicine*, 2009.

Pekka J. Saukko TEFAN POLLOK, "AUTOPSY," IN Wiley Encyclopedia of Forensic Science (JAMIESON, A. & MOENSSENS, A.A., EDS.) 2009 [1] 256.

Gisela Skopp, "Postmortem Toxicology: Artifacts," in WILEY ENCYCLOPEDIA OF FORENSIC SCIENCE (Jamieson, A. & Moenssens, A.A., eds.) 2009 [4] 2093.

Waney Squier, "Shaken Baby Syndrome," in WILEY ENCYCLOPEDIA OF FORENSIC SCIENCE (Jamieson, A. & Moenssens, A.A., eds.) 2009 [5] 2339.

Stefan Timmermans, *Postmortem: How Medical Examiners Explain Suspicious Deaths*, 2006.

Mark D. Viner, "Radiology," in WILEY ENCYCLOPEDIA OF FORENSIC SCIENCE (Jamieson, A. & Moenssens, A.A., eds.) 2009 [5] 2233.

Scott A. Wagner, *Death Scene Investigation*, 2008.

James S. Walker & Bassel Abou–Khalil, "Seizures," in WILEY ENCYCLOPEDIA OF FORENSIC SCIENCE (Jamieson, A. & Moenssens, A.A., eds.) 2009 [5] 2298.

Cyril H. Wecht, book review of Timmermans "Postmortem: How Medical Examiners Explain Suspicious Deaths," 47 JURIMETRICS 251 (2007).

Chapter 15

SEROLOGY AND TOXICOLOGY
OF BODY FLUIDS

III. THE INVESTIGATION OF BLOOD

§ 15.10 Identification of Human Blood Types

Page 989. At the end of the final paragraph of the section, *insert the following additional footnote*:

3. A more comprehensive annotated recent treatment of the subject (with 111 references) is provided in Denise S. Court, "Blood Grouping," in Wiley Encyclopedia of Forensic Science (Jamieson, A. & Moenssens, A.A., eds.) [1] p. 338 (2009).

§ 15.11 Blood Stains

1. TYPES AND COLLECTION

Page 989. At the end of the first paragraph, *insert the following new footnote*:

For a comprehensive recent with significant illustration in color, see: Herbert L. MacDonell, "Bloodstain Pattern Interpretation," in Wiley Encyclopedia of Forensic Science (Jamieson, A. & Moenssens, A.A., eds.) [1] p. 359 (2009).

IV. THE INVESTIGATION OF OTHER
BIOLOGICAL MATTER

Page 993. At the end of the section, *add the following new paragraph*:

§ 15.13 Other Biological Matter in Criminal and Civil Cases

According to the Chapter 5 of the 2009 NAS Report & Scientific Evidence Supplement, biological matters other than blood are located, documented, collected and analyzed at laboratories. These biological materials are more difficult to locate and recognize than average persons would assume. Current techniques for locating these biological materials are identified and explained, including alternative light sources (ALS). Analysis of these materials for the presence of DNA is performed in the laboratory using STR techniques and using CODIS to identify the identity of the person.[1]

---

1. The 2009 NAS Report is discussed in this Supplement, at p. 4.

VII. MISCELLANEOUS

§ 15.23 Bibliography of Additional References

1. GENERAL TOXICOLOGY AND CHEMISTRY

Page 1016. *Insert the following new entries*:

D. Hank Ellison, *Handbook of Chemical and Biological Warfare Agents*, 2nd ed., CRC Press, 2008.

T. Ishikawa *et al.*, "Comparative Evaluation of Postmortem Serum Concentrations of Neopterin and C–Reactive Protein," 179 FORENSIC SCI INT'L 135 (2008).

Richard Li, *Forensic Biology*, CRC Press, 2008.

Peng Liu *et al.*, "Real Time Forensic DNA Analysis at a Crime Scene Using a Portable Microchip Analyzer," 2 FORENSIC SCI. INT'L (2008).

Akemi Marumo *et al.*, "Utility of Disk Solid–Phase Extraction from Whole Blood Samples: Analysis of Some Tetracyclic Antidepressants by Gas Chromatography with Nitrogen–Phosphorus Detection," 26 FORENSIC TOXICOLOGY 13 (2008).

Andre A. Moenssens, "Analysis: Neutron Activation," in WILEY ENCYCLOPEDIA OF FORENSIC SCIENCE (Jamieson, A. & Moenssens, A.A., eds.) [1] 150 (2009).

Bronwyn C. Morrish et al. [6 co-authors], "Chemical, Biological, Radiological and Nuclear Investigations," in WILEY ENCYCLOPEDIA OF FORENSIC SCIENCE (Jamieson, A. & Moenssens, A.A., eds.) [2] 500 (2009).

Keith W. Norman & Victoria C. Gillman, "Chemical Warfare Agents," K. De Wael *et al.*, in WILEY ENCYCLOPEDIA OF FORENSIC SCIENCE (Jamieson, A. & Moenssens, A.A., eds.) [2] 507 (2009).

Andrew S. Robertson, "Biosecurity and International Science," THE SCITECH LAWYER, Winter 2009, p. 12.

S. Seidl *et al.* Comparison of Laser and Mercury–Arc Lamp for the Detection of Body Fluids (2008).

Kelly Virkler & Igor K. Lednev, "Spectroscopy Offers Great Potential for the Nondestructive Confirmatory Identification of Body Fluids," 181 FORENSIC SCI. INT'L e1 (2008).

2. BLOOD GROUPING AND BLOOD ANALYSIS

Page 1017. *Insert the following new entries*

Martin Bauer & Pieter Patzelt, "Identification of Menstrual Blood by Real Time RT–PCR: Technical Improvements and the Practical Value of Negative Test Results," 174 FORENSIC. SCI. INT'L 55 (2008).

Tony Bevel & Ross M. Gardner, *Bloodstain Pattern Analysis with an Introduction to Crime Scene Reconstruction* (3th ed.) 2008.

Herbert L. MacDonell, "Bloodstain Pattern Interpretation," in WILEY ENCYCLOPEDIA OF FORENSIC SCIENCE (Jamieson, A. & Moenssens, A.A., eds.) 2009 [1] 359.

Su Jeong Park *et al.*, "Direct STR Amplification from Whole Blood and Blood-or Saliva-Spotted FTA® without DNA Purification," 53 J. FORENSIC SCIENCES 335 (2008).

Tony Raymond, "Crime Scene Reconstruction from Bloodstains," 29 AUS. J. FORENSIC SCI. 69 (1997).

Brett A. Schweers et al., "Developmental Validation of a Novel Lateral Flow Strip Test for Rapid Identification of Human Blood (Rapid Stain Identification–Blood)," 2 FORENSIC SCI. INT'L (2008)

K. De Wael *et al.*, "In Search of Blood–Detection of Minute Particles Using Spectroscopic Methods," 180 FORENSIC SCI. INT'L 37 (2008).

3. OTHER BIOLOGICAL SUBSTANCES

Page 1018. *Insert the following new entries*:

Anja Fiedler *et al.*, "Detection of Semen (Human and Boar) and Saliva on Fabrics by a Very High Power UV–VIS–Light Source," 1 OPEN FORENSIC SCI. J. 12 (2008).

Daiki Hino *et al.*, "Identification of Sweat Stain Using E-urocanic Acid and L-tyrosine," 13 JAP. J. FORENSIC SCI. AND TECH. 17 (2008).

Jarrah R. Myers & William D. Adkins, "Comparison of Modern Techniques For Saliva Screening," 53 J. FORENSIC SCIENCES 862 (2008).

Chapter 16

DRUGS AND THEIR CONTROL

IV. EVIDENTIAL STATUS OF TEST RESULTS

§ 16.23   General Toxicology Test Results

Page 1068. At the beginning of the section, *insert the following text*:

Chapter 5 of the 2009 NAS Report & Scientific Evidence Supplement, provides information regarding the U.S. Drug Enforcement Administration and Office of National Drug Control Policy, along with the formation of the Scientific Working Group for the Analysis of Seized Drugs (SWGDRUG), which helps develop standards for the analysis of analyzing and reporting of controlled substances. The Report also provides a general summary of the collection procedures and methods of analysis.[1]

VI. TRIAL AIDS

§ 16.28   Bibliography of Additional Materials

Page 1079. *Insert the following additional sources*:

In addition to two articles listed hereafter, the recently published 2009 WILEY ENCYCLOPEDIA OF FORENSIC SCIENCE (Jamieson, A. & Moenssens, A.A., eds.), contains separate articles alphabetically listed under the headings, Amphetamine, Benzodiazepines, Cannabis, Cocaine, Marijuana, and Opioids.

"Campaign to Reform Drug Laws Goes Nationwide" JTO DIRECT, November 15, 2000.

"Speaking Out Against Drug Legalization," www.dea.gov, U.S. Department of Justice May 2003.

Jacquelyn E. Baker & Amanda J. Jenkins, "Screening for Cocaine Metabolite Fails to Detect an Intoxication," 29 AM. J. FORENSIC MED. PATHOLOGY 141 (2008).

Heesung Chung *et al.* [8 co-authors], "Drug Analysis," in WILEY ENCYCLOPEDIA OF FORENSIC SCIENCE (Jamieson, A. & Moenssens, A.A., eds.) 2009 [2] 851.

---

1. The 2009 NAS Report is discussed in Chapter 1 beginning at p. 4, supra.

Edward J. Cone *et al.*, "Urine Drug Testing of Chronic Pain Patients: Licit and Illicit Drug Patterns," 32 J. ANALYTICAL TOXICOLOGY 530 (2008).

Pierre Essava & Pierre Margot, "Drug Profiling," in WILEY ENCYCLOPEDIA OF FORENSIC SCIENCE (Jamieson, A. & Moenssens, A.A., eds.) 2009 [2] 851.

Virginia Hill *et al.*, "Hair Analysis For Cocaine: Factors in Laboratory Contamination Studies and Their Relevance to Proficiency Sample Preparation and Hair Testing," 176 FOR. SCI. INTL. 23 (2008).

Marilyn A. Huestis *et al.*, "Excretion of 9–tetrahydrocannabinol in Sweat," 174 FORENSIC SCI. INT'L 173 (2008).

Subbarao V. Kala *et al.*, "Validation of Analysis of Amphetamines, Opiates, Phencyclidine, Cocaine and Benzoylecqonine in Oral Fluids by Liquid Chromatography–Tandem Mass Spectrometry," 32 J. ANALYTICAL TOXICOLOGY 605 (2008).

Steven B. Karch, *Workplace Drug Testing* (2008).

Steven B. Karch, *Karch's Pathology of Drug Abuse*, 4th ed., 2008.

Jickells, *Clarke's Analytical Forensic Toxicology* (2008).

Robert L. Maginnis, "Hemp is Marijuana: Should Farmers Grow It?" December 2000.

Sandra B. McPherson *et al.*, *Methamphetamine Use: Clinical And Forensic Aspects*, 2d ed. (2008).

Tania A. Sasaki, "Forensic Toxicology Widens Net for Drugs of Abuse— The Rise of LC/MS/NS for Toxicology Testing," FORENSIC MAGAZINE, Oct.–Nov. 2007, p. 20.

Diaa M. Shakleya *et al.*, "Case Report: Trace Evidence of Trans– Phenylpropene as a Marker of Smoked Methamphetamine," 32 J. ANALYTICAL TOXICOLOGY 705 (2008).

B.E. Smink *et al.*, "The Relation between the Blood Benzodiazepine Concentration and Performance in Suspected Impaired Drivers," 15 J. FORENSIC AND LEGAL MED. 483 (2008).

Sandra Thomas *et al.*, "Unusual Fentanyl Patch Administration," 29 AM. J. FORENSIC MED. PATHOLOGY 162 (2008).

Lolita Tsanaclis and John F.C. Wicks, "Differentiation Between Drug Use and Environmental Contamination When Testing for Drugs in Hair," 176 FOR. SCI. INTL. 19 (2008).

Kei Zaitsu *et al.*, "Determination of a Newly Encountered Designer Drug 'p-methoxyethylamphetamine' and Its Metabolites in Human Urine and Blood," 177 FORENSIC SCI. INT'L 77 (2008).

Chapter 17

FORENSIC DNA ANALYSIS—DETERMINING INDIVIDUALITY BY DNA

———

I. INTRODUCTION

§ 17.01   Scope of the Chapter

Page 1083. Paragraph 2 end of first sentence (after "but DNA technology has made leaps and bounds in the field of forensic evidence examination)," *add new footnote*:

See generally Committee on Identifying the Needs of the Forensic Sciences Community, National Research Council, *Strengthening* *Forensic Science in the United States: A Path Forward* (2009).

Page 1084. *Add to footnote 6*:

Although this DNA Index System has restricted access, more information, including a list of participating states and statistics, can be *found at* http://www.fbi.gov/hq/lab/codis/national.htm.

§ 17.02   The Origin of DNA Technology

Page 1086. *Add to footnote 2*:

The Science Photo Gallery URL link, http://www.sciencephotogallery.co.uk/articles/DNA_50yearsArticle.php, for the "Fifty Years of the DNA Double Helix" (1953– 2003) is no longer valid. Similar content is available at http://www.sciencephotogallery.com/pictures_1064420/DNA–50th-Anniversary.html

———

IV.   EVIDENTIARY AND PRACTICAL ASPECTS OF DNA ANALYSIS

§ 17.11   DNA Analysis in the Courts

Page 1113. After the final paragraph of the section, *insert new paragraph in text*:

Moreover, the identification of non-human DNA is becoming increasingly useful in forensic investigations, as highly polymorphic DNA markers become readily available for a wide range of plant and animal species.[1] For example, scientists were able to analyze and identify the

1. See Heather Miller Coyle, *Nonhuman DNA Typing: Theory and Casework Applications* (2007), Kathleen J. Craft et al., "Application of Plant DNA Markers in Fo- rensic Botany: Genetic Comparison of Quercus Evidence Leaves to Crime Scene Trees Using Microsatellites," 165 FORENSIC SCI. INT'L. 64 (2007); Pierre Taberlet et al.,

DNA of dried leaves found in the suspect's car and compare it to the DNA of the same tree species that were growing near a shallow grave where the victims were found.[2] The genetic variation at four microsatellite loci resulting from the DNA analysis was sufficient to assign leaves to an individual tree with high statistical certainty.[3] Consequently, scientists were able to prove the DNA profiles of the dried leaves from the suspect's car did not match those of the trees near the crime scene.[4] Furthermore, the DNA analysis of marijuana plants has been used to identifying the geographic sources of seized drugs.[5] It is expected that non-human DNA forensic evidence will soon become a frequently used tool by both the prosecution and the defense in criminal cases.

Finally, DNA evidence of family members or potential family members is often used in paternity litigation cases. For example, DNA evidence that the affiant was a half-sibling of the deceased mother's son was admissible in support of the claim that the affiant was actually the secret child of the mother and her friend, bond while both were married to other people.[6]

§ 17.12   DNA Evidence as a "Novel Scientific Technique"

Page 1113. At the end of the first sentence, *insert a new footnote*:

See Committee on Identifying the Needs of the Forensic Sciences Community, National Research Council, *Strengthening Forensic Science in the United States: A Path Forward*, 5–3 (2009).

Page 1115. *Add to footnote 11*:

See Christopher Onstott, "Judicial Notice and the Law's 'Scientific' Search for Truth," 40 AKRON L. REV. 465, 491 (2007).

§ 17.14   DNA Database Statute Implementation

Page 1121. *Add to footnote 2*:

Although this DNA Index System has restricted access, more information, including a list of participating states and statistics, can be *found at* http://www.fbi.gov/hq/lab/codis/national.htm.

Page 1122. *Add to footnote 10*:

United States v. Amerson, 483 F.3d 73 (2d Cir.2007) [holding that authorizing collection of DNA samples from felony probation-

"Power and Limitations of the Chloroplast trnL (UAA) Intron for Plant DNA Barcoding," 35 Nucleic Acids Research 14 (2007); Cheng–Lung Lee et al., "DNA Analysis of Digested Tomato Seeds in Stomach Contents," 27 AM. J. FORENSIC MED. & PATHOLOGY 121 (2006).

2. Kathleen J. Craft et al., "Application of Plant DNA Markers in Forensic Botany: Genetic Comparison of Quercus Evidence Leaves to Crime Scene Trees Using Microsatellites," 165 FORENSIC SCI. INT'L. 64 (2007).

3. *Id.*

4. *Id.*

5. Shannon L. Datwyler & George D. Weiblen, "Genetic Variation in Hemp and Marijuana (Cannabis sativa L.) According to Amplified Fragment Length Polymorphisms," 51 J. FORENSIC SCI. 371 (2006).

6. In re Estate of Gaynor, 13 Misc.3d 331, 818 N.Y.S.2d 747 (Sur. Ct. 2006).

ers does not constitute an unreasonable search or seizure as applied to probationers convicted of nonviolent crimes]; *also see Johnson v. Quander*, 440 F.3d 489 (D.C.Cir. 2006) [holding that the Fourth Amendment does not prohibit the government from storing probationer's DNA].

Page 1122. *Add to footnote 11*:

United States v. Amerson, 483 F.3d 73 (2d Cir.2007) [holding that probationers have a diminished expectation of privacy, both immediate and long-term, from DNA testing; while "the government has a compelling interest in using DNA database to rapidly and accurately solve crimes ..."].

Page 1123. *Add to footnote 12*:

State v. O'Hagen, 189 N.J. 140, 914 A.2d 267 (2007) [addressing the "special needs" analysis].

Page 1123. *Add to footnote 14*:

United States v. Reynard, 473 F.3d 1008 (9th Cir.2007) [holding that the retroactive application of the DNA Act, such as the requirement that a defendant on supervised release provide a blood sample for a government database, does not violate *ex post facto* laws].

1. COLD CASES

Page 1125. *Add to footnote 19*:

People v. Nelson, 142 Cal.App.4th 696, 48 Cal.Rptr.3d 399 (3d Dist.2006) [the Court allowed the DNA evidence in a murder case, which was identified in a cold hit profiling match with biological evidence from the crime scene, because the scientific community has generally accepted random match probability in DNA databank cases].

Page 1125. *Add to footnote 21*:

Jackson v. State, 92 Md.App. 304, 608 A.2d 782 (1992), cert. denied 328 Md. 238, 614 A.2d 84 [The State is not required to offer additional evidence where the DNA testing has been legislatively determined to be reliable and generally admissible, and where standard procedures and equipment were utilized in the conducting of the DNA analysis].

Page 1125. *Add to footnote 22*:

Molina v. Commonwealth, 272 Va. 666, 636 S.E.2d 470 (2006) [DNA evidence was sufficient to support a conviction of forcible sodomy].

§ 17.16   Recent Bibliography [New]

Beginning on page 1126, after "Conclusion," *insert the following new paragraphs*:

1. ARTICLES AND JOURNALS

Scott Bader, "Hardy–Weinberg Equilibrium," in WILEY ENCYCLOPEDIA OF FORENSIC SCIENCE (Jamieson, A. & Moenssens, A.A., eds.) 2009 [3] 1458.

John S. Buckleton, "Mixture Interpretation," in WILEY ENCYCLOPEDIA OF FORENSIC SCIENCE (Jamieson, A. & Moenssens, A.A., eds.) 2009 [4] 1838.

Robert Berlet, "A Step Too Far: Due Process and DNA Collection in California after Proposition," 40 U.C. DAVIS L. REV. 1481 (2007).

Michael Booth, "Court Sustains Constitutionality of Mandatory DNA Sampling Statute," N.J.L.J. (January 24, 2007).

Michael J. Coble & Rebecca S. Just, "Mini–STRs,"in WILEY ENCYCLOPEDIA OF FORENSIC SCIENCE (Jamieson, A. & Moenssens, A.A., eds.) 2009 [4] 1804.

B. Michael Dann et al., "Can Jury Trial Innovations Improve Juror Understanding of DNA Evidence?," 90 JUDICATURE 152 (2007).

Susan E. Davis, "Buried in DNA: despite Hype about Using DNA to Break Unsolved Crimes, Cold Case Units Face Slow Going," 27 CAL. LAW. 13 (2007).

Troy Duster, "Explaining Differential Trust of DNA Forensic Technology: Grounded Assessment or Inexplicable Paranoia," 34 J.L. MED. & ETHICS 293 (2006).

Kirsten Edwards, "Cold Hit Complacency: the Dangers of DNA Databases Re–Examined," 18 CURRENT ISSUES CRIM. JUST. 92 (2006).

Sepideh Esmaili, "Searching for a Needle in a Haystack: the Constitutionality of Police DNA Dragnets," 82 CHI.-KENT L. REV. 495 (2007).

Paul C. Giannelli, "Forensic Science: Under the Microscope," 34 OHIO N.U.L. REV. 315 (2008).

Paul C. Giannelli, "Science for Judges VII: Evaluating Evidence of Causation & Forensic Laboratories: Current Issues & Standards: Regulating Crime Laboratories: The Impact of DNA Evidence," 15 J.L. & POL'Y 59 (2007).

Jason R. Gilder, "DNA: Degraded Samples," in WILEY ENCYCLOPEDIA OF FORENSIC SCIENCE (Jamieson, A. & Moenssens, A.A., eds.) 2009 [2] 816.

Eleanor A. M. Graham, "DNA: An Overview," in WILEY ENCYCLOPEDIA OF FORENSIC SCIENCE (Jamieson, A. & Moenssens, A.A., eds.) 2009 [2] 800.

Henry T. Greely et al., "Family Ties: The Use of DNA Offender Databases to Catch Offenders' Kin," 34 J.L. MED. & ETHICS 248 (2006).

Mark Hamblett, "Circuit Approves Taking DNA Samples from Nonviolent Felons on Probation," N.Y. L.J. (April 6, 2007).

Mark Hansen, "DNA Poised to Show Its Civil Side," ABA JOURNAL, Mar. 2008, p. 18.

Sally Ann Harbison, "DNA: Sources of," in WILEY ENCYCLOPEDIA OF FORENSIC SCIENCE (Jamieson, A. & Moenssens, A.A., eds.) 2009 [2] 820.

Joshua Hillel Hubner, "Blinded by Science: Does the General Acceptance of Forensic DNA Evidence Warrant a More Streamlined Approach to Admissibility," 18 U. FLA. J.L. & PUB. POL'Y 93 (2007).

Vesna Jaksic, " 'Abandoned DNA' triggers new debate over privacy" NAT'L L.J. 2007 WL 1506551 (2007).

Tonja Jacobi & Gwendolyn Carroll, "Acknowledging Guilt: Forcing Self–Identification in Post-conviction DNA Testing," 102 Nw. U.L. REV. 263 (2008).

Allan Jamieson, "DNA Transfer," in WILEY ENCYCLOPEDIA OF FORENSIC SCIENCE (Jamieson A. & Moenssens A.A., eds.) 2009 [5] 2555.

Elizabeth E. Joh, "Reclaiming 'Abandoned' DNA: the 4th Amendment and Genetic Privacy," 100 Nw. U. L. REV. 857 (2006).

Frederika A. Kaestle et al., "Database Limitations on the Evidentiary Value of Forensic Mitochondrial DNA Evidence," 43 AM. CRIM. L. REV. 53 (2006).

D. H. Kaye, "Who Needs Special Needs? On the Constitutionality of Collecting DNA and Other Biometric Data from Arrestees," 34 J.L. MED. & ETHICS 188 (2006).

David H. Kaye, "The Science of DNA Identification: from the Laboratory to the Courtroom (and Beyond)," 8 MINN. J. L. SCI. & TECH. 409 (2007).

Michael E. Kleinert, "Improving the Quality of Justice: the Innocence Protection Act of 2004 Ensures Post-conviction DNA Testing, Better Legal Representation, and Increased Compensation for the Wrongfully Imprisoned," 44 BRANDEIS L.J. 491 (2006).

Dan E. Krane, "Low Copy Number DNA," in WILEY ENCYCLOPEDIA OF FORENSIC SCIENCE (Jamieson, A. & Moenssens, A.A., eds.) 2009 [3] 1639.

Tracey Maclin, "Is Obtaining an Arrestee's DNA a Valid Special Needs Search under the 4th Amendment? What Should (and Will) the Supreme Court Do," 34 J.L. MED. & ETHICS 165 (2006).

Terry Melton, "Mitochondrial DNA: Profiling," in WILEY ENCYCLOPEDIA OF FORENSIC SCIENCE (Jamieson, A. & Moenssens, A.A., eds.) 2009 [4] 1833.

Paul M. Monteleoni, "DNA Databases, Universality, and the Fourth Amendment," 82 N.Y.U. L. REV. 247 (2007).

Thomas J. Moyer, Chief Justice, "Biotechnology and the Bar: A Response to the Growing Divide Between Science and the Legal Environment," 22 BERKELEY TECH. L.J. 671 (2007).

Matthew J. Mueller, "Handling Claims of Actual Innocence: Rejecting Federal Habeas Corpus As the Best Avenue for Addressing Claims of Innocence Based on DNA Evidence," 56 CATH. U. L. REV. 227 (2006).

Erin Murphy, "The New Forensics: Criminal Justice, False Certainty, and the 2nd Generation of Scientific Evidence," 95 CAL. L. REV. 721 (2007).

David R. Paoletti et al., "Assessing the Implications for Close Relatives in the Event of Similar but Nonmatching DNA Profiles," 46 JURIMETRICS J.L. SCI. & TECH. 161 (2006).

Julie Rikelman, "Justifying Forcible DNA Testing Schemes under the Special Needs Exception to the 4th Amendment: A Dangerous Precedent," 59 BAYLOR L. REV. 41 (2007).

Tania Simoncelli & Barry Steinhardt, "California's Proposition 69: a Dangerous Precedent for Criminal DNA Databases," 34 J.L. MED. & ETHICS 199 (2006).

Julie A. Singer et al., "The Impact of DNA and Other Technology on the Criminal Justice System: Improvements and Complications," 17 ALB. L.J. SCI. & TECH. 87 (2007).

Deborah Sulzbach, "DNA Shall Prevail: Postconviction DNA Evidence: an Annotated Bibliography," 25 LEGAL REFERENCE SERV. Q. 39 (2006).

Katie L. Swango et al., "A Quantitative PCR Assay for the Assessment of DNA Degradation in Forensic Samples," 158 FORENSIC SCI. INT'L 14 (2006).

Robert Tanner, "DNA Taken from Those Arrested More Frequently," 152 CHI. DAILY L. BULL. 1 (2006).

Sophia Tareen, "DNA Leads to Release of Man Who Served 25 Years for Rape," 153 CHI. DAILY L. BULL. 1 (2007).

Gillian Tully & Jon Wetton, "Mitochondrial DNA: Interpretation," in WILEY ENCYCLOPEDIA OF FORENSIC SCIENCE (Jamieson, A. & Moenssens, A.A., eds.) 2009 [4] 1823.

Simon J. Walsh & John Buckleton, DNA "Databases and Evidentiary Issue," in WILEY ENCYCLOPEDIA OF FORENSIC SCIENCE (Jamieson, A. & Moenssens, A.A., eds.) 2009 [2] 1458.

Simon J. Walsh, "DNA: an Overview," in WILEY ENCYCLOPEDIA OF FORENSIC SCIENCE (Jamieson, A. & Moenssens, A.A., eds.) 2009 [2] 792.

Robin Williams & Paul Johnson, "Inclusiveness, Effectiveness and Intrusiveness: Issues in the Developing Uses of DNA Profiling in Support of Criminal Investigations," 34 J.L. MED. & ETHICS 234 (2006).

2. BOOKS

ABA Standards for Criminal Justice: DNA Evidence (2007).

Jay D. Aronson, *Genetic Witness: Science, Law, and Controversy in the Making of DNA Profiling* (2007).

George Clarke, *Justice and Science: Trials and Triumphs of DNA Evidence* (2008).

Heather Miller Coyle, *Nonhuman DNA Typing: Theory and Casework Applications* (2007).

Peter Gill, *Principles of DNA Profiling* (2008).

Daniel L. Hartl & Elizabeth W. Jones, *Genetics: Analysis of Genes and Genomes* (2008).

Jacquie T. Keer & Lyndsey Birch, *Essentials of Nucleic Acid Analysis: A Robust Approach* (2008).

Terrence F. Kiely, *Forensic Evidence: Science and the Criminal Law* (2006).

Lawrence F. Kobilinsky, *Forensic DNA Analysis* (2008).

Richard Li, *Forensic Biology: Identification and DNA Analysis of Biological Evidence* (2008).

Thomas J. McClintock, *Forensic DNA Analysis: a Laboratory Manual* (2008).

Ron C. Michaelis et al., *A Litigator's Guide to DNA: From the Laboratory to the Courtroom* (2008).

Sabine Müller, *Nucleic Acids from A to Z: A Concise Encyclopedia* (2008).

David E. Newton, *DNA Evidence and Forensic Science* (2008).

Elizabeth van Pelt–Verkuil, *Principles and Technical Aspects of PCR Amplification* (2008).

Ralph Rapley & *David Whitehouse, Molecular Forensics* (2007).

Andrei Semikhodskii, *Dealing with DNA Evidence: A Legal Guide* (2007).

Paul Singleton, *Dictionary of DNA and Genome Technology* (2008).

Tim Thompson & Sue M. Black, *Forensic Human Identification: An Introduction* (2006).

Victor W. Weedn & R. E. Gaensslen, *Handbook of Forensic DNA Typing* (2007).

Robin Williams & Paul Johnson, *Genetic Policing: The Use of DNA in Criminal Investigations* (2008).

Chapter 18

FORENSIC ODONTOLOGY

III. EVIDENCE OF DENTAL IDENTIFICATION

§ 18.07 Evidence of Bite Mark Identifications

Page 1152. *Add the following paragraphs to the end of the section*:

Mississippi dentist Michael West testified in 72 trials between 1988 and 2002 as a bite mark identification expert, mostly for Southern prosecutors.[1] West had an uncanny ability to see things that his colleagues could not and this ability often led to convictions. West frequently told defense attorneys in court that his bite mark identification error rate was "something less than my savior, Jesus Christ."[2]

West also uses what he calls the "West Phenomenon," a method he invented which involves yellow goggles and a blue laser. He claims he can identify bite marks, scratches, and other tissue imperfections on a corpse that are invisible to everyone else, including other bite mark experts. He has allegedly found bite marks on bodies that had been submerged in swamps for weeks, and on corpses that had been buried for over a year.[3]

Using the "West Phenomenon," West claimed to have found bite marks on a decomposed woman's breast that previous pathologists had missed.[4]

West used his method in another case where he claimed to have positively traced a half-eaten sandwich at the crime scene to the defendant. The defendant was convicted, but the case was later tossed out when West admitted to disposing of the sandwich after studying it. West claimed the sandwich was no longer necessary because no other expert could replicate his methods.[5]

West swore under oath at a trial in 1995 that a dead girl had bite marks all over her body made by Kennedy Brewer's two front teeth. A

---

1. Jim Fisher, *Forensics Under Fire: Are Bad Science and Dueling Experts Corrupting Criminal Justice?* (2008).

2. *Mark Hanson*, "Out of the Blue," 82 *ABA* J. 50 (1996).

3. Radley Balko, "Faulty Forensic 'Experts' Sending the Innocent to Jail," Fox-News.com, Aug. 3, 2007, found at www.foxnews.com/story/0,2933,291452,00.html (last checked on Dec. 13, 2008).

4. Id.

5. Id.

---

jury convicted Brewer and sentenced him to death for raping and murdering the 3–year-old girl.[6]

Brewer was exonerated in February 2008 when a man confessed to the killing after DNA connected him to the rape.[7] Forensic experts examining the Brewer case said the victim's wounds were not human bites but rather were probably caused by a combination of crawfish and insects nibbling on the corpse, decomposition, and rough handling when the body was pulled from the pond where it was found.[8]

This was not the first time a conviction assisted by West's testimony had been reversed.

West examined an exhumed body in 1992 and found a bite mark wound on the corpse's shoulder using his blue light. The bite mark had not shown up on any crime scene or autopsy photographs. Sheriff's deputies arrested the victim's ex-husband when West matched the blue light-enhanced bite mark to a cast of the man's dentition.

At trial the jury had to rely on West's testimony because the blue light image could not be photographed. The judge denied a defense motion to exclude West's testimony. Subsequently the jury convicted the victim's ex-husband. In 1994, a Louisiana appeals court set aside the conviction on grounds that the trial judge had erred in admitting West's testimony. The victim's ex-husband was not retried because the only evidence against him was the bite mark.[9]

Also in 1994, Mississippi prosecutors dropped charges against Johnny Bourn, who had been in jail for 18 months awaiting trial for allegedly raping and robbing a woman. Bourn was arrested after West identified him as the source of a bite mark found on the victim. DNA, fingerprint, and hair evidence exonerated Bourn and charges were dropped.[10]

Other odontologists have also assisted in convictions, only to see them overturned when additional forensic evidence proved the dental identifications erroneous.[11]

Michael Bowers, an odontologist and lawyer who served on the examination and credentialing committee of the American Board of Forensic Odontology, co-wrote a 2002 study that estimated the performance of board-certified odontologists in a workshop exercise. Bowers estimated that board-certified odontologists falsely identified an innocent person as the biter nearly two-thirds of the time.[12]

In 2007, Eric Frimpong, an immigrant from Ghana who played soccer at UC Santa Barbara, was charged with raping a UCSB coed on a

6. Sheila Byrd, "2 Men Freed in Child Death Bite–Mark Cases," Associated Press, Feb. 29, 2008.

7. Id.

8. Id.

9. *Mark Hanson*, "Out of the Blue," 82 *ABA* J. 50 (1996).

10. Id.

11. Jim Fisher, *Forensics Under Fire: Are Bad Science and Dueling Experts Corrupting Criminal Justice?* (2008).

12. Flynn McRoberts and Steve Mills, "From the Start, a Faulty Science: Testimony on Bite Marks Prone to Error," Chicago Trib., Oct. 19, 2004.

beach. Forensic dentist Norman Sperber testified that a bite mark on the rape victim's buttocks and cheek could have been inflicted by Frimpong.[13] He also testified he could rule out that the victim's boyfriend made the bite based on a mold taken of the boyfriend's mouth.[14]

The defense attorney said moldings taken of the victim's boyfriend's teeth were not provided to the defense until after Sperber's testimony, despite having requested them months earlier.[15] The defense attorney also claimed that he was unable to call its own expert dentist because his expert, Michael Bowers, was ill when he was supposed to testify. The attorney claimed that after the trial Bowers concluded his analyses on the teeth moldings and victim's bite marks and found that Frimpong likely did not inflict the bites.[16] At a retrial hearing, Bowers offered testimony that directly contradicted Sperber's. Bowers said he believed the bite mark on the victim's cheek showed bottom teeth on the side nearest her mouth and top teeth away from her mouth, the opposite of Sperber's conclusions.[17]

Semen found in the victim's underwear was positively identified as belonging to her boyfriend.[18] Despite this evidence, a jury convicted Frimpong of rape and he was sentenced to six years in prison.

IV. MISCELLANEOUS

§ 18.10 Bibliography of Additional References

Herman Bernitz, Johanna H. Owen, Willie F.P. van Heerden, & Tore Solheim, "An Integrated Technique for the Analysis of Skin Bite Marks," 53 J. FORENSIC SCIENCES 194 (2008).

Christina Cataneo & Danilo De Angelis, "Odontology" in WILEY ENCYCLOPEDIA OF FORENSIC SCIENCE (Jamieson, A. & Moenssens, A.A., eds.) 2009 [4] 1889.

Paul C. Giannelli, "Bite Mark Evidence," CRIM. JUSTICE, Spring 2007, p. 42.

R. F. Kouble & G. T. Craig, "A Survey of the incidence of Missing Anterior Teeth: Potential Value in Bite Mark Analysis," 47 SCIENCE AND JUSTICE 19 (2007).

Debra A. Prince, Erin H. Kimmerloe & Lyle W. Konigsberg, "A Bayesian Approach to Estimate Skeletal Age-at-Death Utilizing Dental Wear," 53 J. FORENSIC SCIENCE 588 (2008).

---

13. Colby Frazier, "Attorney Requests New Trial for Convicted Rapist," DAILY SOUND, Jan. 31, 2008.

14. Chris Meagher, "Defense's Case Winds Down," SANTA BARBARA INDEPENDENT, Dec. 13, 2007.

15. Chris Meagher, "Judge Hears Frimpong's Retrial Motion," SANTA BARBARA INDEPENDENT, Feb. 28, 2008.

16. Id.

17. Id.

18. Id.

Todd Richmond, "Scientists are building database of bite marks," at YAHOO! NEWS, http://news.yahoo.com/s/ap/20080514/ap on re us/bite marks ... (last visited on May 19, 2008).

Chapter 19

FORENSIC ANTHROPOLOGY

Page 1157. *Change* **footnote * to:**

* Catherine M. Bailey, J.D. is a member of the Florida Bar and is a Research Attorney for the National Clearinghouse for Science, Technology and the Law at Stetson University College of Law. The contents of this chapter are the views of its primary author and this text's co-authors. The opinions, findings and conclusions, or recommendations expressed in this chapter do not necessarily reflect the views of the Department of Justice, the National Institute of Justice, the National Clearinghouse for Science, Technology and the Law, Stetson University, or Stetson University College of Law. The authors wish to thank Heather Walsh–Haney, Ph.D., Forensic Anthropologist and Assistant Professor, Florida Gulf Coast University, for her review of this chapter and for her insightful comments and suggestions.

I. INTRODUCTION

§ 19.01 Scope of the Chapter

Page 1159. At the end of footnote 2, *add the following*:

In 2008 modern practitioners examined the evolution of forensic anthropology over the past twenty years and concluded that the specialty had expanded greatly beyond its original focus of victim and trauma identification. These scholars thus broadly defined forensic anthropology as "the scientific discipline that focuses on the life, the death, and the postlife history of a specific individual, as reflected primarily in their skeletal remains and the physical and forensic context in which they are emplaced." Dennis C. Dirkmaat, at al., "New Perspectives in Forensic Anthropology," 51 Yearbook Phys. Anthr. 33 at 47 (2008).

§ 19.02 The Origins of Forensic Anthropology

Page 1160. *Change footnote 2 to*:

See the AAFS website at http://www.aafs.org, last viewed December 1, 2008.

Page 1160. *Change the last sentence of footnote 3 to*:

See also the ABFA website at http://www.csuchico.edu/anth/ABFA, last viewed December 1, 2008.

Page 1160. *Change footnote 4 to*:

See James E. Starrs, "The Erumpent Quality of Bones in Forensic Science," 17(3) Sci. Sleuthing Rev. (1993) and 18(1) Sci. Sleuthing Rev. (1994), analyzing many of these appellate court decisions. A recent review of relevant case law shows that this figure can be updated to over 125 cases. This number refers to the number of individual cases (excluding subsequent appeals of the same case) wherein the appellate opinion clearly reflected the introduction, or attempted introduction, of testimony from a physical or forensic anthropologist.

Page 1162. In the second full paragraph beginning with "There are two ...", *change sixth sentence to*:

The FDB contains over 2900 cases, more than 1800 of which involve definite ancestry and sex.

Page 1162. *Change the third full paragraph beginning with "The second development is the ..." to*:

The second development is the creation of the Anthropological Research Facility (ARF), also at the University of Tennessee, Knoxville. The project, envisioned and developed by forensic anthropologist and professor Dr. William M. Bass, is "the world's first ... laboratory devoted to the study of human decomposition." ARF, also known as the Body Farm, began with one acre of land wherein students and scientist could monitor and study donated bodies as they decayed under various conditions. The first subject was donated in 1981 and by 2008 almost 650 corpses had been studied at the facility. This resulted in not only in new anthropological discoveries, but also "some of the first systematic findings of forensic entomology ... as well as the ... discipline of estimating time of death from the chemical breakdown of body fluids leaching from a decomposing corpse." A similar field laboratory recently opened at Western Carolina University in Cullowhee, North Carolina, and comparable facilities have been proposed in other states such as Texas.

Page 1162. *Change footnote 19 to*:

Byers, supra note 3, at 8; See also the FDB website at http://web.utk.edu/?fac/databank.shtml, last viewed December 1, 2008.

Page 1162. *Change footnote 20 to*:

Id.

Page 1162. *Change footnote 21 to*:

See also the FDB website at http://web.utk.edu/?fac/databank.shtml, last viewed December 1, 2008.

Page 1162. *Change footnote 26 to*:

Id.; Jessica Sachs, "No Scientist Knows More about Time of Death than Bill Bass," Leg. Aff. (2004); http://web.utk.edu/?fac/facilities.shtml, last viewed December 1, 2008.

Page 1162. *Add footnote 27a*:

27a. See the homepage for the Western Carolina Human Identification Laboratory at http://www.wcu.edu/3409.asp, last viewed December 1, 2008. According to the Forensic Anthropology Center at Texas State website, Texas State University announced in February of 2008 that it would build its Forensic Research Facility on a 3,000–acre ranch San Marcos, Texas, http://www.txstate.edu/anthropology/facts, last viewed December 1, 2008.

§ 19.03   The Purposes of Forensic Anthropology

Page 1163. At the end of footnote 3, *add*:

See also Cristina Cattaneo, "Forensic Anthropology: Developments of a Classical Discipline in the New Millennium," 165 FORENSIC SCI. 185 (2007), explaining that anthropology has recently been used to: age juvenile perpetrators, determine whether images in pornography are of children versus adults, and identify bank robbers caught on film. See for example A. Schmeling, et al., "Age Estimation," 165 FORENSIC SCI. INT'L 178 (2008) explaining that "estimation of living persons has formed a relatively recent area of forensic research which is becoming increasingly important."

Page 1163. *Change footnote 5 to*:

See the discussion in "Identifying the Perpetrator," infra § 19.11(4).

II.   IDENTIFICATION

§ 19.04   The Process of Identification: In General

Page 1164. At the end of footnote 3, *add*:

See also F. Dedouit, et al., "Virtual Anthropology and Forensic Identification: Report of One Case," 173 FORENSIC SCI. INT'L 182 (2007) and T.J. Thompson & J.A. Chudek, "A Novel Approach to the Visualisation of Heat–Induced Structural Change in Bone," 47 SCIENCE & JUSTICE 99 (2007).

2.   IS IT HUMAN?

b.   MICROSCOPIC METHOD

Page 1167. At the end of footnote 21, *add*:

See also M.L. Hillier & L.S. Bell, "Differentiating Human Bone from Animal Bone: A Review of Histological Methods," 52 J. FORENSIC SCI. 249 (2007).

§ 19.05   General or Class Characteristics of Human Bone

Page 1173. *Change* the first sentence of footnote 1 to:

Robert J. Terry Anatomical Skeletal Collection, Department of Anthropology, National Museum of Natural History, Smithsonian Institution, http://www.nmnh.si.edu/anthro/cm/terry.htm, last viewed December 1, 2008;

1.   ESTIMATION OF AGE AT DEATH

a.   SUB–ADULTS

Page 1175. *Add* to the end of footnote 11:

Anthropologists have also proposed a new, related technique involving mandibular measurements of sub-adults. D. Franklin & A. Cardini, "Mandibular Morphology As an Indicator of Human Subadult Age: Interlandmark Approaches," 52 J. FORENSIC SCI. 1015 (2008).

Page 1176. *Add* to the end of footnote 18:

See also C. Rissech, et al., "Development of the Femur—Implications for Age and Sex Determination," 180 Forensic Sci. Int'l 87 (2008).

b. ADULTS: MICROSCOPIC METHODS

Page 1177. *Add* to the end of footnote 25:

See also: G. González–Colmenares, at al., "Age Estimation by a Dental Method: A Comparison of Lamendin's and Prince & Ubelaker's Technique," 52 J. Forensic Sci. 1156 (2008)

c. Adults: Macroscopic Methods

Page 1179. *Add* to the end of footnote 28:

But see: Sharma, et al., "Determination of Age from Pubic Symphysis: An Autopsy Study," 48 Med. Sci. & Law 163 (2008).

Page 1180. *Add* to the end of footnote 31:

But see: G.E. Burge, "Pubic Bone Age Estimation in Adult Women," 53 J. Forensic Sci. 569 (2008) suggesting "the need for a new phase, phase VII, that follows the Suchey–Brooks phase VI."

2. DETERMINATION OF SEX

a. Pelvic Features, Gross Morphological Assessment (Adult)

Page 1185. *Add* to the end of footnote 60:

See also K.R. Nagesh, "Sexual Dimorphism of Acetabulum–Pubis Index in South–Indian Population," 9 Leg. Med. 305 (2007).

b. Other Features, Gross Morphological Assessment

Page 1185. *Add* to the end of footnote 61:

See also: E.H. Kimmerle, et al., "Sexual Dimorphism in America: Geometric Morphometric Analysis of the Craniofacial Region," 53 J. Forensic Sci. 54 (2008).

c. Mathematical Assessment

Page 1186. *Change footnote 62 to*:

http://web.dii.utk.edu/fordisc, last viewed December 2, 2008.

e. Post-Cranial Bones

Page 1187. *Add* to the end of footnote 71:

For information about using skeletal foot/toe characteristics to determine sex, see: R.H. Abdel Had, et al., "Identification of Sex Depending on Radiological Examination of Foot and Patella," 29 Am. J. Forensic Med. Path. 136 (2008) and R. Moudgil, et al., "Foot Index: Is It a Tool for Sex Determination," 15 J. FORENSIC LEG. & MED. 223 (2008).

3.   DETERMINATION OF ANCESTRY

Page 1189. *Change the second sentence in footnote 86 to*:

See the American Anthropological Association Statement on Race at http://www. aaanet.org/stmts/racepp.htm, posted May 17, 1998 and last viewed December 2, 2008;

4.   DETERMINATION OF STATURE

a.   LONG BONE MEASUREMENT: REGRESSION EQUATIONS

Page 1195. *Add* to the end of footnote 105:

See also M.H. Raxter, et al., "Revision of the Fully Technique for Estimating Statures," 130 AM. J. PHYS. ANTHR. 374 (2006); T. Kanchan, et al., "Stature Estimation from Foot Dimensions," 179 FORENSIC SCI. INT'L 241 (2008).

§ 19.06   **Individualization of Human Bone**

2.   VARIABILITY OF CERTAIN BONES

Page 1198. *Add* to the end of footnote 3:

See also C.P. Campobasso, et al., "Craniofacial Identification by Comparison of Antemortem and Postmortem Radiographs: Two Case Reports Dealing with Burnt Bodies," 28 AM. J. FORENSIC MED. & PATH. 182 (2007).

3.   PHOTOGRAPHIC SUPERIMPOSITION

Page 1200. *Add* to the end of footnote 19:

See also H. Eliásová & P. Krsek, "Superimposition and Projective Transformation of 3D Object," 167 FORENSIC SCI. INT'L 146 (2007).

4.   FACIAL RECONSTRUCTION

Page 1200. *Change* the second sentence in footnote 22 to:

See also Caroline Wilkinson, *Forensic Facial Reconstruction* (2004) and G. Quatrehomme, et al., "Assessment of the Accuracy of Three–Dimensional Manual Craniofacial Reconstruction: A Series of 25 Controlled Cases," 121 INT'L J. LEG. MED. 469 (2007).

Page 1201. *Add* to the end of footnote 24:

S. de Greef, et al., "Large–Scale In–Vivo Caucasian Facial Soft Tissue Thickness Database for Craniofacial Reconstruction," 159 FORENSIC SCI. INT'L SUPPL. S126 (2006); J.M. Starbuck & R.E. Ward, "The Affect of Tissue Depth Variation on Craniofacial Reconstructions," 172 FORENSIC SCI. INT'L 130 (2007).

Page 1201. *Add* to the end of footnote 26:

P. Claes, et al., "Craniofacial Reconstruction Using a Combined Statistical Model of Face Shape and Soft Tissue Depths: Methodology and Validation," 159 FORENSIC SCI. INT'L SUPPL. S147 (2006); W.D. Turner, et al., "A Novel Method of Automated Skull Registration for Forensic Facial Approximation," 154 FORENSIC SCI. INT'L 149 (2005).

III. CAUSE AND MANNER OF DEATH

§ 19.07 Signs of Trauma

Page 1202. *Change* **footnote 2 to:**

Michael J. Thali, et al., "Into the Decomposed Body: Forensic Digital Autopsy Using Multislice–Computed Tomography," 134 FORENSIC SCI. INT'L 109 (2003). The creators of the virtual autopsy, known as Virtopsy, have helped to pioneer this methodology. For more information about this development in death investigation, see http://www.virtopsy.com, last viewed December 3, 2008. See also J. C. Myers, et al., "Three-dimensional (3–D) Imaging in Post-mortem Examinations: Elucidation and Identification of Cranial and Facial Fractures in Victims of Homicide Utilizing 3–D Computerized Imaging Reconstruction Techniques," 113 INT'L J. LEG. MED. 33 (1999); and F. Dedouit, et al., supra note 3, § 19.04.

2. GUNSHOT INDUCED TRAUMA TO BONE

Page 1202. *Add* **to the end of footnote 3:**

See also N.R. Langley, "An Anthropological Analysis of Gunshot Wounds to the Chest," 52 J. FORENSIC SCI. 532 (2007).

5. SHARP FORCE TRAUMA

Page 1206. *Add* **to the end of footnote 19:**

See also A.M. Croft & R. Ferllini, "Macroscopic Characteristics of Screwdriver Trauma," 52 J. FORENSIC SCI. 1243 (2007); P. A. Saville, S. V. Hainsworth & G. N. Rutty, "Cutting Crime: The Analysis of the 'Uniqueness' of Saw Marks on Bone," 121 INT'L. J. LEG. MED. 349 (2007); V. Alunni–Perret et al., "Scanning Electron Microscopy Analysis of Experimental Bone Hacking Trauma," 50 J. FORENSIC SCI. 796 (2005); Michael J. Thali et al., "Forensic Microradiology: Micro–Computed Tomography (Micro–CT) and Analysis of Patterned Injuries Inside of Bone," 48 J. FORENSIC SCI. 1336 (2003).

IV. EVIDENCE OF ANTHROPOLOGICAL EXAMINATIONS

§ 19.08 The Current State of the Art

Page 1207. *Change paragraph beginning with "A review of all reported ..." to:*

A review of all reported decisions from both state and federal courts through late–2008 wherein the testimony of physical anthropologists was mentioned confirms the more widespread and crucial involvement of such experts in the courtroom in recent years. These decisions, which numbered about 50 in 1993 and over 125 by late 2008, generally reveal courts' ready approval of the scientific standing of the opinions of physical or forensic anthropologists.

Page 1208. *Change* **footnote 10 to:**

http://www.fox.com/bones, last viewed December 3, 2008.

Page 1208. *Change* **footnote 11 to:**

http://www.cbs.com/primetime/csi, last viewed December 3, 2008.

Page 1208. *Change* **footnote 12 to:**

http://www.atlasmediacorp.com/buzz/buzz. php?id=88, last viewed December 3, 2008.

§ 19.09　Qualifying the Expert

1.　THE NON–FORENSIC ANTHROPOLOGIST

b.　Medical Professionals Who Are Not Anthropologists

Page 1212. *Add* **to the end of footnote 19:**

See also Gilson v. Sirmons, 520 F.3d 1196, 1201 (10th Cir.2008) wherein a medical examiner testified that, although he could not determine cause of death from skeletal remains, he was able to draw conclusions about the timing and nature of the victim's injuries, which included several fractures.

2.　THE FORENSIC ANTHROPOLOGIST

Page 1213. *Change* **footnote 28 to:**

For more information on this subject see "Identifying the Perpetrator," infra § 19.11(4).

Page 1214. *Change* **footnote 32 to:**

Dellinger v. State, 2007 WL 2428049, *17 (Tenn.Crim.App.2007).

Page 1214. *Change* **footnote 37 to:**

Klindt, supra note 36, at 673; For more examples of opinions wherein admitted forensic anthropological testimony is referenced with little to no analytical discussion see: Mangialino v. White Haven Memr'l. Park, 132 A.D.2d 970, 518 N.Y.S.2d 532 (1987); State v. Balfa, 506 So.2d 1369, 1370 (La.App.1987); Bassett v. State, 449 So.2d 803 (Fla.1984); People v. Ellis, 188 A.D.2d 1043, 592 N.Y.S.2d 200 (1992); State v. Nielsen, 946 A.2d 382 (Me.2008); Major v. McDaniel, 2008 WL 1777830 (D.Nev.2008); and Rhodes v. State, 986 So.2d 501 (Fla. 2008).

Page 1215. *Add* **to the end of footnote 44:**

But see Clemons v. Commonwealth, 2006 WL 2986532, *1 (Ky.2006) wherein the forensic anthropologist testified that the victim's body had been moved around after burning. This opinion actually did reflect the basis for this conclusion because it included the explanatory statement that "skull fragments were found beneath the buttocks."

Page 1215. *Change* **footnote 47 to:**

Ellis, supra note 37.

Page 1216. *Change* **footnote 48 to:**

State v. Goodman, 643 S.W.2d 375 (Tenn. Crim.App.1982); State v. Hartman, 703 S.W.2d 106 (Tenn.1985); See generally "Identifying the Deceased," infra § 19.11.

Page 1216. *Add* **to the end of footnote 49:**

See also "The Forensic Anthropologist as a Team Player" infra § 19.11(1) and "The Evidential Value of Insects in the Criminal Context" infra § 19.11(5) for additional examples of anthropologists performing more than just skeletal analysis. See also Esty v. McDonough, 2007 WL 1294602 (N.D.Fla. 2007) wherein the court suggests that a particular forensic anthropologist's testimony about outdoor decomposition rates could have been excluded for lack of scientific reliability under a Frye analysis of admissibility. This is not to say that anthropologists can never become an authority in other fields through additional training and experience. Perhaps this was the case in Janoushek v. Watkins, 2007 WL 2316947 (D.Colo.2007) wherein the court received a forensic anthropologist as a forensic trichology (hair and fiber) expert.

§ 19.10   Demonstrative Evidence: Bones in the Courtroom

Page 1219. *Change* **footnote 17 to:**

Supra note 43, § 19.09.

§ 19.11   Legal Uses for the Forensic Anthropologist

1.   THE FORENSIC ANTHROPOLOGIST AS A TEAM PLAYER

Page 1220. *Change* **footnote 2 to:**

Hollis, supra note 43, § 19.09; Hartman, supra note 48, § 19.09.

Page 1220. *Add* **to the end of footnote 3:**

See also, Koestler v. Koestler, 976 So.2d 372, 382 (Miss.App.2008) wherein "a forensic pathologist testified that a forensic anthropologist was present during an autopsy and that the forensic anthropologist's comments were 'confirmatory' of his findings. [The pathologist] also testified that the forensic anthropologist's comments were 'something that is reasonably and customarily relied upon by forensic pathologists . . . in forming opinions'."

Page 1221. *Add* **to end of footnote 9:**

Anthropologists have also provided evidence to support the medical examiners' conclusions about wounding instrumentalities. For example, in State v. Robinson, 2008 WL 2700002, *7–8 (Ohio App.2008) a forensic anthropologist determined that the victim's mandible "contained a small, diamond-shaped defect. From this examination, [the anthropologist] was able to discern that the tip of the weapon that caused the defect had a point; that the weapon had to be fairly sturdy in order to puncture the hard, dense bone of the mandible; and that the weapon had a 'rounded flattened diamond shape at the tip cross section'." The anthropologist then went further and confirmed the forensic pathologist's conclusion that a letter opener, or one just like it, had created the wound. However anthropologists usually will refrain from making definite conclusions about a specific weapon. For example see Reedy v. State, 214 S.W.3d 567 (Tex. App.—Austin 2006) wherein a forensic anthropologist testified "I don't know if that [hatchet] caused the trauma or another hatchet caused the trauma. What this appears is that the trauma was caused by an implement that had a right angle and that was approximately 20 to 22 millimeters in diameter as is that hatchet." Forensic anthropologists can also support other patho-logical findings such as malnutrition, as seen in Commonwealth v. Robidoux, 450 Mass. 144, 877 N.E.2d 232, 239 (2007).

Page 1221. *Add* footnote 10a after footnote 10:

10a. Forensic anthropologists have also provided evidence about physical crime scenes in order to support, or in some cases even refute, conclusions from other forensic specialists such as CSI technicians, reconstructionists and entomologists. For example in Holt v. State a forensic anthropologist testified about an arson scene, explaining that the young victim had been underneath her "bed as opposed to being on top, because the chain [used to restrain her] was not draped over the top of the bedframe." 2007 WL 1697316, *1 (Ark. App.2007). See also Carruthers v. State, 2007 WL 4355481 (Tenn.Crim.App.2007) wherein a forensic anthropologist testified about the order of burial of multiple bodies, and State v. Hughes, 2007 WL 1319373, *1 (Tenn.Crim.App.2007) wherein "Dr. Lee Jantz, a forensic anthropologist, stated that the body was fully clothed and wrapped in a rug."

3.   PROVING THE CORPUS DELICTI

Page 1223. *Change* footnote 22 to:

For example see Caudill, supra note 5, § 19.10, Johnson v. Campbell, 2007 WL 3144709, *3 (N.D.Cal.2007), State v. Wright, 839 So.2d 1112, 1117 (La.App. 2003), and Pipkin, supra note 34, § 19.09, at *3.

a.   IDENTIFYING THE DECEASED

Page 1223. *Change* footnote 23 to:

2008 WL 1823072 (Conn.Super.2008).

Page 1223. *Add* to the end of footnote 24:

Note that in State v. Miraballes, 392 N.J.Super. 342, 920 A.2d 736 (App.Div. 2007) an anthropologist was apparently able to positively identify multiple victims from skeletal remains found in a basement, though her analytical process was not explained in the opinion.

Page 1223. *Add* to the end of footnote 25:

See also Sock v. Trombley, 2006 WL 2711506, *8 (E.D.Mich.2006), wherein "a biologic anthropologist, compared the remains with a 1979 x-ray of Minnella's spinal column and positively identified the fragments of three vertebrae as being the victim's. He also observed that the x-ray showed a fracture in rib number seven that was consistent with a fracture callous on the fragment of rib number seven among the remains."

Page 1223. *Change* the first sentence in footnote 28 to:

Supra note 32, § 19.09.

Page 1223. *Add* to the end of footnote 29:

For more examples of anthropologists providing estimations on age, race, stature and/or sex see: State v. Bruce, 2008 WL 3971088 (Ohio App.2008), Wilkins v. State, 286 Kan. 971, 190 P.3d 957 (2008), Mashburn v. State, 272 S.W.3d 1 (Tex.App.— Fort Worth 2008), People v. Goff, 2008 WL 2266138 (Cal.App.2008), People v. Mayns, 2008 WL 2212370 (Cal.App.2008), State v. Bryant, 2008 WL 544650 (Tenn.Crim.App. 2008), Horn v. Quarterman, 508 F.3d 306 (5th Cir.2007), State v. Horton, 283 Kan. 44, 151 P.3d 9 (2007), and Lewis v. State,

2008 WL 2736894, *3 (Tex.Crim.App.2008). Interestingly in the Lewis case the forensic anthropologist went so far as to testify that: "that the victim had 'fairly powerful hands'."

Page 1224. *Add* to the end of footnote 32:

See also Day v. Commonwealth, 2006 WL 2707960, *1 (Ky.2006) wherein the state forensic anthropologist was allowed to testify that "time of death was 3 to 10 months before the remains were found." The anthropologist made sure to qualify her testimony by also explaining that "it could have been earlier-it was very difficult to tell given the varying condition of the remains," Dirago v. Hendricks, 2005 WL 3113429, *18 (D.N.J.2005) wherein "a defense expert anthropologist ... testified that the victim's remains had been present at the discovery site for no more than three months before its discovery," and Gore v. Secretary for Dept. of Corrections, 492 F.3d 1273 (11th Cir.2007) wherein a forensic anthropologist testified that "the body could have been in the ... woods anywhere from two weeks to six months before it was discovered, but that a two to four month range was the most likely scenario." But see Gell v. Town of Aulander, 2008 WL 4845823, *2 (E.D.N.C.2008) wherein a forensic anthropologist specified a very narrow window for the time of death when he stated that the victim died "on or about April 9, 1995."

Page 1224. *Add* to the end of footnote 38:

See also Cristina Cattaneo, "Forensic Anthropology: Developments of a Classical Discipline in the New Millennium," 165 FORENSIC SCI. INT'L. 185, 188 (2007), explaining that: "[Crano-facial reconstruction] ... should be used only to stimulate the memory of the public in order to reach a suspicion of identity."

b.   IDENTIFYING THE CRIMINAL CAUSE OF DEATH

Page 1226. *Change second sentence in paragraph beginning with "Even though a ..." to*:

As explained in State v. Bobby, "if the trauma, for instance a bullet, does not directly impact the bones it does not show up on the skeletal remains."

Page 1226. *Add* to the end of footnote 44:

See also Lovin v. State, 2007 WL 1946667, *3 (Tenn.Crim.App.2007), and State v. Tallant, 2008 WL 115818, *3 (Tenn.Crim.App. 2008).

Page 1226. *Change* footnote 46 to:

2007 WL 2427999, *4 (N.D. Ohio 2007).

Page 1227. *Add* to the end of footnote 49:

See also: State v. Ward, 2007 WL 1556663 (Tenn.Crim.App.2007) wherein the forensic anthropologist's "examination of the head and neck of the left femur indicated there had been an attempt to cut off the left leg," Whipple v. State, 281 S.W.3d 482, 493 (Tex. App.—Austin 2008) wherein a forensic anthropologist "determined that the long bone fragments and vertebrae fragments had been cut with some type of manual saw with a straight blade approximately one millimeter wide. In his opinion, a hacksaw found in Appellant's garage was consistent with the class of saws that could have been used to cut the bones," and State v. Bryant, 2008 WL 544650, *12 (Tenn.Crim.App. 2008) wherein the forensic anthropologist testified that "some of the impacts from the blade, which was 12/100 of an inch in width, slit open the bone and some of the hacking marks appeared to have been an attempt to dismember the body."

Page 1227. *Add* **to the end of footnote 53:**

See also State v. Jones, 2007 WL 1946654, *2 (Tenn.Crim.App.2007).

Page 1228. *Change* **footnote 57 to:**

For example see People v. St. Pierre, 122 Ill.2d 95, 118 Ill.Dec. 606, 522 N.E.2d 61 (1988); Bassett v. State, 449 So.2d 803 (Fla. 1984); Elliott, supra note 43, at 283, Bryant, supra note 49.

Page 1228. *Change* **footnote 65 to:**

Smith, supra note 46, *4.

4. IDENTIFYING THE PERPETRATOR

b. THE ANALYSIS OF FOOT AND SHOE PRINTS

Page 1233. *Change* **footnote 95 to:**

166 Cal.App.3d 46, 212 Cal.Rptr. 307 (1985).

5. THE EVIDENTIAL VALUE OF INSECTS IN THE CRIMINAL CONTEXT

Page 1235. *Change* **footnote 114 to:**

For an in depth discussion of the field of forensic entomology see *Forensic Entomology: The Utility of Arthropods in Legal Investigations*, Second Edition (Jason H. Byrd & James L. Castner, eds. 2009); *Forensic Entomology: An Introduction* (Dorothy Gennard, 2007); *Entomology and Death: A Procedural Guide*, Spiral Edition (E. Paul Catts & Neal Haskell, eds., 1990).

Page 1236. *Add* **to the end of the fourth sentence in footnote 116:**

and Gore v. Secretary for Dept. of Corrections, 492 F.3d 1273, 1286 (11th Cir.2007) wherein a forensic anthropologist testified that: "... the extreme decomposition of the left breast indicated that there may have been an injury to that area, making it the easiest target for insects."

Page 1236. *Add* **to the end of footnote 117:**

Note also that entomologists, like any other forensic specialists, can testify either for the prosecution or as an expert for the defense. For example, see Richie v. Sirmons, 563 F.Supp.2d 1250, 1285 (N.D.Okla.2008), Bayer v. State, 2008 WL 516692, *3 (Tex. App.—Texarkana 2008), and Rummer v. State, 722 N.W.2d 528 (N.D.2006) wherein defendants hired expert entomologists to dispute the time of death. See also Thorson v. State, 994 So.2d 707, *9 (Miss.2007) and Dellinger v. State, 2007 WL 2428049, *8–9 (Tenn.Crim.App.2007). An entomologist's testimony can also be used to refute the state's conclusions about the *cause* of death, as seen in Stocker v. State, 2007 WL 1435391, *2 (Tex.App.—Amarillo 2007). Additionally entomologists may be called to testify in civil cases that involve insect activity, such as infestation and food spoliation trials. For example, see Grogan v. Gamber Corp., 19 Misc.3d 798, 858 N.Y.S.2d 519, 523 (N.Y.Sup.2008).

Page 1236. *Add* **to the end of footnote 118:**

See also Clemons v. Commonwealth, 2006 WL 2986532, *1 (Ky.2006) wherein the forensic anthropologist testified that "... based upon the life stage of the insects, ...

it had been 4–7 days since the fire," and Wilson v. Parker, 515 F.3d 682, 689 (6th Cir.2008), wherein "[a] forensic entomologist testified that, based on the extent of blowfly maggot development in and on the corpse, the estimated time of death had occurred 15 to 19 days prior to his June 16 examination of the corpse."

Page 1236. *Add* **to the end of footnote 120:**

See also Stevens v. McBride, 489 F.3d 883, 906 (7th Cir.2007) wherein "[t]he forensic entomologist who examined insect samples found in the body and in the soil under the bridge placed the time of death sometime between noon and sunset on July 15."

Page 1237. *Change* **footnote 129 to:**

Id. For another example of an entomologist who discovered possible errors in her conclusions during trial, see Stutelberg v. State, 741 N.W.2d 867, 870 (Minn.2007).

Page 1239. *Add* **to the end of footnote 129:**

See also Gell v. Town of Aulander, 2008 WL 4845823, *3 (E.D.N.C.2008) wherein the defendant did "not object to the qualifications or methodologies of the date of death experts," including a forensic entomologist.

Page 1240. *Add* **to the end of footnote 145:**

But while this may be true, there is still room for professionals in these fields to disagree with one another on specific cases. For example, see Dellinger, note 117, at *17 wherein well-known and board certified forensic entomologist, Dr. Neal Haskell, refuted entomological testimony from famed anthropologist Dr. William Bass. Haskell explained "there was a distinct difference in the two fields in that the anthropologist would study the bones while the entomologist would study aspects of insect behavior."

Page 1240. *Add* **to the end of footnote 149:**

Such entomological testimony was again challenged in Esty v. McDonough, 2007 WL 1294602, *27–28 (N.D.Fla.2007). In this case testimony from anthropologist Dr. Rodriguez (it is unclear whether this is same Dr. Rodriguez from the aforementioned Michael Miller case) was introduced by the prosecution to bolster conclusions from the state's forensic pathologist about the victim's time of death, and to rebut evidence submitted by two defense experts, a forensic entomologist and an associate medical examiner. On appeal the defendant claimed he received ineffective assistance of counsel because his attorney failed to properly challenge the Rodriguez's testimony. The appellate court agreed with defendant that his attorney should have requested a hearing on the admissibility of Rodriguez's conclusions because it was likely that they would not have survived a *Frye* analysis and thus would have been excluded. However the appellate court pointed out that Rodriguez's testimony did not prejudice the defendant because the anthropologist's statements were "equivocal, cumulative and largely ineffectual," and in fact even undermined the state's own case. There was also sufficient additional evidence to convict defendant.

6.   INVESTIGATING HUMAN RIGHTS VIOLATIONS

Page 1241. *Add* **to the end of footnote 150:**

See also *Forensic Approaches to Death, Disaster and Abuse* (Marc Oxenham, 2008).

Page 1241. *Change* **footnote 151 to:**

See the International Covenants on Human Rights (1976), which include the International Covenant on Economic, Social and Cultural Rights and the International Covenant on Civil and Political Rights; See also the United Nations Convention against

Torture and Other Cruel, Inhuman, or Degrading Treatment or Punishment; See also http://www.amnesty.org, last viewed December 8, 2008. See also H. McKelvie & B. Loff, "Human Rights, Controls, and Principles," *Encyclopedia of Forensic and Legal Medicine; Volume 2*, 538 (Jason Payne–James, et al., eds., 2005) for a discussion of International Humanitarian Law (IHL).

Page 1241. *Change* **footnote 152:**

See the American Anthropological Association Committee for Human Rights' website at http://www.aaanet.org/committees/cfhr/index.htm, last viewed December 8, 2008. See also scientific journal articles such as Erin H. Kimmerle, et al., "Skeletal Estimation and Identification In American and East European Populations," 53 J. FORENSIC SCI. 524 (2008), and texts such as *Skeletal Trauma: Identification of Injuries Resulting from Human Rights Abuse and Armed Conflict* (Erin H. Kimmerle, Jose Pablo Baraybar, 2008).

Page 1241. *Add* **to the end of footnote 153:**

See also *Recovery, Analysis, and Identification of Commingled Human Remains* (Bradley J. Adams and John E. Byrd, eds., 2008), M. Djuric, et al., "Identification of Victims from Two Mass–Graves in Serbia: A Critical Evaluation of Classical Markers of Identity," 172 FORENSIC SCI. INT'L. 125 (2007), and M. Djuirc & H. Tuller, "Keeping the Pieces Together: Comparison of Mass Grave Excavation Methodology," 156 FORENSIC SCI. INT'L. 192 (2006).

7. THE FORENSIC ANTHROPOLOGIST IN CIVIL TRIALS

Page 1243. *Change* **the first sentence of footnote 160 to:**

Such as Hurricane Katrina in 2005 and the Thailand Tsunami in 2004. For example, see the Louisiana Family Assistance Center (FAC) website at http://www.dhh.louisiana.gov/offices/?ID=303, last viewed December 9, 2008.

Page 1243. *Change* **the last sentence of footnote 161 to:**

This non-profit group evolved into DMORT as it is known today. See http://dmort.org, last viewed December 9, 2008.

Page 1246. *Add* **to the end of footnote 166:**

For another life insurance policy case, see Mitchell v. Globe Life and Acc. Ins. Co., 548 F.Supp.2d 1385, 1389 (N.D.Ga.2007) wherein the medical examiner solicited an anthropological consultation, though it proved to be "unrevealing."

———

V.   TRIAL AIDS

§ 19.12   Locating and Selecting a Forensic Anthropologist

Page 1247. *Change the paragraph that begins with "The American Academy of . . ." to:*

The American Academy of Forensic Sciences lists 411 persons as being affiliated in various categories of membership in its Section of Physical Anthropology. 107 of those listed are student members. 62 have successfully completed the professional and examination requirements of the American Board of Forensic Anthropology, an arm of the Forensic

Sciences Foundation, and have the privilege of describing themselves as Diplomates.

Page 1247. *Change* **footnote 1 to:**

Personal communication, 2008. The contact information for AAFS is: 410 North 21st Street, Colorado Springs, CO 80904, Telephone: (719) 6361100, Fax: (719) 636–1993, Website: http://www.aafs.org, last viewed December 9, 2008. As explained in Englert v. MacDonell, 2006 WL 1310498, *1 (D.Or. 2006), "Courts frequently recognize membership in [the American Academy of Forensic Science] as an indicator of the professional qualifications necessary to qualify an expert witness in forensic science."

Page 1247. *Change* **footnote 2 to:**

250 South Stadium Hall, Knoxville, TN, 37996–0720, Telephone: (865) 974–4408, Fax: (865) 974–2686, Website: http://web. utk.edu/?anthrop/, last viewed December 9, 2008.

Page 1247. *Change* **footnote 4 to:**

2200 Wilson Boulevard, Suite 600, Arlington, VA 22201, Telephone: (703) 528–1902, Fax: (703) 528–3546 Website: http://www. aaanet.org, last viewed December 9, 2008.

Page 1247. *Change* **footnote 5 to:**

Website: http://www.physanth.org, last viewed December 9, 2008.

VI. MISCELLANEOUS

§ 19.13   Bibliography and Additional References

Page 1247. *Add the following to the bibliography and list of additional resources*:

Bill Bass & Jon Jefferson, *Beyond the Body Farm: A Legendary Bone Detective Explores Murders, Mysteries, and the Revolution in Forensic Science* (2007).

Gregory E. Berg, "Pubic Bone Age Estimation in Adult Women," 53 J. FORENSIC SCIENCES 569 (2008).

Megan B. Brickley & Roxana Ferllini, eds. *Forensic Anthropology: Case Studies from Europe* (2007).

Steven N. Byers, *Introduction to Forensic Anthropology: A Textbook*, 3rd Edition (2007).

Jason H. Byrd & James L. Castner, eds., *Forensic Entomology: The Utility of Arthropods in Legal Investigations*, 2nd Edition (2009).

Cristina Cattaneo, "Anthropology: Age Determination of Remains," in WILEY ENCYCLOPEDIA OF FORENSIC SCIENCE (Jamieson, A. & Moenssens, A.A., eds.) 2009 [1] 179.

Cristina Cattaneo, "Anthropology: Aging the Livins," in WILEY ENCYCLOPEDIA OF FORENSIC SCIENCE (Jamieson, A. & Moenssens, A.A., eds.) 2009 [1] 188.

Christina Cattaneo, "Anthropology: Ancestry and Stature Determination," in WILEY ENCYCLOPEDIA OF FORENSIC SCIENCE (Jamieson, A. & Moenssens, A.A., eds.) 2009 [1] 191.

Christina Cattaneo & Daniele Gibelle, "Postmortem Interval: Anthropology," in WILEY ENCYCLOPEDIA OF FORENSIC SCIENCE (Jamieson, A. & Moenssens, A.A., eds.) 2009 [4] 2089.

Cristina Cattaneo & Davide Porta, "Facial Reconstruction," in WILEY ENCYCLOPEDIA OF FORENSIC SCIENCE (Jamieson, A. & Moenssens, A.A., eds.) 2009 [3] 1086.

Todd W. Fenton, Amber N. Heard & Norman J. Sauer, "Skull–Photo Superimposition and Border Deaths: Identification through Exclusion and the Failure to Exclude," 53 J. FORENSIC SCIENCES 34 (2008).

Diane L. France, *"Human and Nonhuman Bone Identification—A Color Atlas, 2008 Dorothy Gennard," Forensic Entomology: An Introduction* (2007).

Erin H. Kimmerle, Ann Ross & Dennis Slice, "Sexual Dimorphism in America: Geometric Morphometric Analysis of the Craniofacial Region," 53 J. FORENSIC SCIENCES 54 (2008).

Erin H. Kimmerle, Lyle W. Konigsberg, Richard L. Janz & Jose Pablo Baraybar, 53 J. FORENSIC SCIENCES 57 (2008).

Marc Oxenham, *Forensic Approaches to Death, Disaster and Abuse* (2008).

Patrick Randolph–Quinnie, Zanthe Mallett & Sue Black, in WILEY ENCYCLOPEDIA OF FORENSIC SCIENCE (Jamieson, A. & Moenssens, A.A., eds.) 2009 [1] 152. [Extensively annotated with 214 references.]

Robert B. Pickering & David Bachman, *The Use of Forensic Anthropology*, 2nd ed. 2009.

Arnout C. C. Ruifrok, "Facial Comparison," in WILEY ENCYCLOPEDIA OF FORENSIC SCIENCE (Jamieson, A. & Moenssens, A.A., eds.) 2009 [3] 1081.

Christopher W. Schmidt & Steven Symes, *The Analysis of Burned Human Remains* (2008).

Mark Tibbett & David O. Carter, *Soil Analysis in Forensic Taphonomy: Chemical and Biological Effects of Buried Human Remains* (2008).

Heather A. Walsh–Haney, et al., *The Forensic Anthropology Laboratory* (2008).

Michael W. Warren, Laurel Freas & Heather A. Walsh–Haney, *The Forensic Anthropology Laboratory*, 2008.

Michael Warren & Nicolette Parr, *Bare Bones: A Survey of Forensic Anthropology* (2008).

*

Part IV

BEHAVIORAL SCIENCE EVIDENCE[1]

Chapter 20

BEHAVIORAL SCIENCES AND THE LAW

———

I. INTRODUCTION

§ 20.01   Scope of the Chapter

Page 1255. *Add to footnote 3*:

See also, D. Shuman, S. Greenberg, K. Heilbrun, W. Foote, Special Perspective: An Immodest Proposal: Should Treating Mental Health Professionals Be Barred from Testifying about Their Patients, *Behavioral Sciences & the Law*, 16, 509–523 (1998).

§ 20.02   The Origins of Social Science and Law

Page 1256. *Update to footnote 4*:

John Monohan & Laurens Walker, *Social Science in the Law: Cases and Materials* (6th ed. 2006).

Page 1257. *Add to footnote 10*:

APLS now sponsors a student section website, *available at* http://www.aplsstudentsection.com (last visited November 21, 2008).

§ 20.03   Social Science and Law Today

Page 1258. *Add to footnote 2*:

An invited article was also written 13 years later reflecting on the original work in C. Haney (1993). Psychology and legal change: The impact of a decade. *Law and Human Behavior*, 17, 371–398.

§ 20.05   Some Common Psychiatric and Psychological Terms and Their Meaning

Add to list of terms:

Asperger's Disorder: Pervasive developmental disorder in which there is a substantial delay in social interaction and a development of

———

1. Assisting in the supplementation of the materials in Chapters 20 through 23 were: Amanda Hardy, Diana Manee, Shanna Fox Oakley, and Darcy Wallus, The University of North Carolina at Charlotte.

restricted, repetitive patterns of behavior, interests, and activities. However, language, curiosity, and cognitive development proceed normally.

Autistic Disorder: Pervasive developmental disorder with onset prior to age 3 in which there is a qualitative impairment in social interaction and communication associated with restricted, repetitive and stereotyped patterns of behavior. There is also a delay in at least one of the following areas: 1) social interaction, 2) language as used in social communication, or 3) symbolic or imaginative play.

Add to CAT Scan: Sometimes known as "CT scan."

fMRI: Functional Magnetic Resonance Imaging: Specialized form of MRI that measures regulation of blood flow in the brain. This tool has become increasingly popular due to its low invasiveness.

MMSE: Mini–Mental State Examination: Brief and widely used measure of cognitive status in adults that was created in 1975 and is now published by Psychological Assessment Resources, Inc. It is most often used as a screening tool for cognitive impairment, but may also be used to measure severity of impairment or to document change in cognitive status over time.

MSE: Mental Status Examination: Clinical assessment used to determine if an individual is suffering from a mental impairment. It can include the examiner's observations about the individual's appearance, behavior, affect, speech, thought process, insight, and judgment.

Update to Wechsler Adult Intelligence Scale (WAIS): This test is now in its 3rd edition and known as the WAIS–III.

Wechsler Intelligence Scale for Children—Fourth Edition (WISC–IV): Psychological diagnostic test to measure intelligence and mental retardation in children, ages 6–16, consisting of standardized full scale IQ, verbal memory, working memory, perceptual reasoning, and processing speed scores.

III. FORENSIC PSYCHIATRY

§ 20.10 The Profession of Psychiatry

Page 1278. *Update to footnote 1:*

Its address is: American Psychiatric Association, 1000 Wilson Boulevard, Suite 1825 Arlington VA, 22209.

§ 20.11 Types of Psychiatric Disorders

Page 1279. *Add to paragraph 1:*

The DSM uses a multi-axial system to diagnose clients on five axes or categories of functioning. Axis I consists of mental disorders and other disorders that may be the focus of clinical attention. Axis II consists of underlying pervasive conditions including personality disorders and mental retardation. Axis III consists of medical conditions and physical disorders. Axis IV consists of contributing psychosocial and environmental factors. On axis V clinicians report a Global Assessment of Functioning or GAF score which ranges from 1 (severely impaired functioning) to 100 (superior functioning) a score of 0 indicates there is not enough information to provide a GAF score. Children under the age of 18 are given a Children's Global Assessment Scale or CGAS score which also ranges from 1 to 100.

Page 1279. *Add to footnote 1:*

There are over 120 scientific researchers and clinicians who are working to develop the DSM–V which is expected to be published in May 2012. These professionals have been divided into 13 workgroups that are expected to reflect the 13 diagnostic categories for the DSM–V. The current focuses of the individual workgroups are ADHD and Disruptive Behavior Disorders; Anxiety, Obsessive–Compulsive Spectrum, Posttraumatic, and Dissociative Disorders; Childhood and Adolescent Disorders; Eating Disorders; Mood Disorders; Neurocognitive Disorders; Neurodevelopmental Disorders; Personality and Personality Disorders; Psychotic Disorders; Sexual and Gender Identity Disorders; Sleep–Wake Disorders; Somatic Distress Disorders; Substance–Related Disorders. While these categories are similar to the classification system for the DSM–IV–TR, it is predicted that they will evolve to reflect the most recent research findings.

§ 20.13 Examination of the Patient/Client

5. DIAGNOSTIC CLASSIFICATION

Page 1287. *Update to footnote 3:*

The 6th edition of *Coping with Psychiatric and Psychological Testimony* was expected to be released in March 2009.

Page 1287. *Add to footnote 4:*

R. Rosenthal (1994). Science and Ethics in Conducting, Analyzing, and Reporting Psychological Research. *Psychological Science*, 5, 127–134.

R. MacCoun (1998). Biases in the Interpretation and Use of Research Results. *Annual Review of Psychology*, 49, 259–287.

K. Sterba (2006). Misconduct in the Analysis and Reporting of Data: Bridging Methodological and Ethical Agendas for Change. *Ethics & Behavior*, 16, 305–318.

Page 1287. *Add to footnote 5:*

See also, D. Shuman, S. Greenberg, K. Heilbrun, W. Foote, Special Perspective: An Immodest Proposal: Should Treating Mental Health Professionals Be Barred from Testifying about Their Patients, *Behavioral Sciences & the Law*, 16, 509–523 (1998).

IV. PSYCHOLOGY AND LAW

§ 20.16 Expert Qualifications and Roles of Clinical Psychologists

Page 1295. *Add to footnote 2:*

For examples of common ethical dilemmas faced by forensic psychologists and a model for ethical decision making, see, S. Bush, M. Connell, & R. Denney (2006) *Ethical Practice in Forensic Psychology: A Systematic Model for Decision Making.*

§ 20.17 Psychological Testing Devices

1. PERSONALITY TESTS

Page 1298. *Add to footnote 1:*

MMPI–2: Assessing Personality and Psychopathology by John R. *Graham* (4th ed. 2005).

Page 1298. *Add to footnote 2:*

Also see, J. Verela, M. Boccaccini, F. Scogin, J. Stump, & A. Caputo (2004) Personality Testing in Law Enforcement Employment Settings *Criminal Justice and Behavior*, 31, 649–675.

Page 1299. *Add to paragraph 3:*

There is also the Millon Clinical Multiaxial Inventory—III (MCMI–III), the most commonly used self-report personality disorder inventory. It is divided into five sections measuring moderately severe personality pathologies, severe personality pathologies, moderate clinical syndromes (i.e. DSM–IV–TR Axis I Disorders), severe clinical syndromes, and modifying factors (e.g. tendency to underreport symptoms). This inventory should *only* be used for individuals who are believed to have a personality disorder, since it will always produce a clinically significant score.

Page 1299. *Add to footnote 4:*

Also see, H. Garb, J. Wood, S. Lilienfeld, M. Nezworski (2004) Roots of the Rorschach controversy *Clinical Psychology Review*, 25, 97–118.

Page 1300. *Update to footnote 5:*

See, Leopold Bellak and David M. Abrams *The T.A.T., The C.A.T., and The S.A.T. in Clinical Use*, 1996, currently in its 6th edition.

2. INTELLIGENCE TESTS

Page 1301. *Add to the second paragraph under "Intelligence Tests":*

The Wechsler Intelligence Scale for Children—Fourth Edition (WISC–IV) is also commonly used for children ages 6–16. For children ages 2 years 6 months to 7 years three months, the Wechsler Preschool and Primary Scale of Intelligence—Third Edition (WPPSI–III) may also be used.

————

V. FORENSIC NEUROLOGY AND NEUROPSYCHOLOGY

§ 20.20 Some Organic Neurological Disorders

Page 1308. *Add to paragraph 3, line 8*:

The newest and increasingly most popular instrument is functional magnetic resonance imaging (fMRI) which provides a structural and functional view of the brain based on blood flow. This instrument offers a high resolution image with low invasiveness.

§ 20.21 Neurological and Neuropsychological Examinations

Page 1310. *Update to footnote 3*:

The Wechsler Adult Intelligence Scale (WAIS) is now in its 3rd Edition (WAIS–III).

The Wechsler Memory Scale (WMS) is now in its 3rd Edition (WMS–III).

The Wide Range Achievement Test (WRAT) is now in its 4th Edition (WRAT–IV).

Page 1310. *Add to footnote 3*:

Neuropsychologists also use the Test of Memory Malingering (TOMM) to distinguish between truly impaired individuals and malingerers.

————

VII. TRIAL PRACTICE

§ 20.24 Locating the Expert

1. THE PSYCHIATRIST

Page 1312. *Update to footnote 1*:

The address of the American Psychiatric Association is 1000 Wilson Boulevard, Suite 1825 Arlington VA, 22209.

Page 1313. *Update to footnote 2*:

The American Board of Forensic Psychiatry disbanded in 1994 and the American Board of Psychology and Neurology began certifying forensic psychiatrists. Persons holding this certification are now entitled to use the designation, "Certification in the Subspecialty of Forensic Psychiatry."

3. THE NEUROLOGIST

Page 1314. *Update to footnote 5*:

The address of the American Neurological Association is 5841 Cedar Lake Road, Suite 204, Minneapolis, MN 55416.

§ 20.25 Ethical Dilemmas of the Expert Witness

Page 1314. *Add footnote 1*:

1. For a discussion on the ethical dilemmas of the expert witness see, S. Greenberg D. Shuman (1997) *Irreconcilable conflict between therapeutic* and *forensic* roles. Professional Psychology: Research & Practice, 28, 50–58; and D. Shuman, S. Greenberg, K. Heilbrun, W. Foote, Special Perspecitve: An Immodest Proposal: Should Treating Mental Health Professionals Be Barred from Testifying about Their Patients, *Behavioral Sciences & the Law*, 16, 509–523 (1998).

VIII. MISCELLANEOUS

§ 20.26 Bibliography of Additional References

1. BOOKS

Page 1315. *Update list of books*:

Anon., *Diagnostic and Statistical Manual of Mental Disorders (DSM–IV–TR)*. The DSM–V is expected to be published in 2012.

Paul S. Applebaum & Thomas Gutheil, *Clinical Handbook of Psychiatry and the Law*, 4th ed. 2006.

F.J. Gravetter & L.B. Wallnau, *Statistics for the Behavioral Sciences*, 6th ed., 2006.

Jan E. Leestma, *Forensic Neuropathology*, 2nd ed. (2008).

E.G. Phares, *Clinical Psychology: Concepts, Methods, and Profession*, 6th ed., 2001.

Robert J. Waldinger, *Psychiatry for Medical Students*, 3rd ed. 1997.

2. ARTICLES

The recently released WILEY ENCYCLOPEDIA OF FORENSIC SCIENCE (Jamieson, A. & Moenssens, A.A., eds.), 2009, contains over 90 articles as part of its Behavioral Science section. Because the volumes were not yet received at the time this Supplement was prepared, no mention of specific articles contained in its 5 volumes is attempted. The print edition is also expected to become available in 2010 in online format and updated annually.

Chapter 21

EXPERT EVIDENCE ON INSANITY AND OTHER MENTAL HEALTH CONDITIONS

II. THE DEFENSE OF INSANITY AND RELATED CONCEPTS

§ 21.02   Insanity as a Defense to Crime

1.   THE M'NAGHTEN TEST

Page 1323. *Update to footnote 4:*

General Principles of Criminal Law is still in its second edition, but was reprinted by The Lawbook Exchange Ltd. in 2005.

6.   MODERN CONCEPTUAL CHANGES

Page 1326. *Add to footnote 16:*

Also see, Insanity Defense Workgroup (1984). American Psychiatric Association Statement on the Insanity Defense *American Journal of Psychiatry*, 140, 161–168.

Also see, J.J. Mcgrath (1984). Toward unity: The joint statement of the American Medical Association and the American Psychiatric Association regarding the insanity defense. *American Journal of Psychiatry*, 142, 1058–1059.

Page 1327. *Add to footnote 18:*

For an overview of the Yates case as it relates to postpartum psychosis see, D. West, B. Lichtenstein (2006). Andrea Yates and the Criminalization of the Filicidal Maternal Body. *Feminist Criminology*, 1, 173–187.

7.   MYTHS ABOUT THE INSANITY DEFENSE

Page 1327. *Add to footnote 19:*

Also see, A. L. Bloechl, M. J. Vitacco, C. S. Neumann and S. E. Erickson (2007). An empirical investigation of insanity defense attitudes: Exploring factors related to bias *International Journal of Law and Psychiatry*, 30, 153–161.

§ 21.03   Psychiatric and Psychological Evidence of Insanity

1.   DISSOCIATIVE IDENTITY DISORDER, FORMERLY MULTIPLE PERSONALITY DISORDER (MPD)

Page 1328. *Add to paragraph 1, line 5*:

Dissociative Identity Disorder is part of a cluster of disorders known as Dissociative Disorders, which are characterized by disruption in awareness, identity, consciousness, and memory. Other Dissociative Disorders in the DSM–IV–TR include Dissociative Amnesia, Depersonalization Disorder, and Dissociative Fugue.

2.   POSTPARTUM PSYCHOSIS

Page 1331. *Add to paragraph 2, line 5*:

Postpartum psychosis differs from postpartum depression mostly in that the former is a psychotic disorder, while the latter is a mood disorder. Postpartum depression occurs when the mother's symptoms meet diagnostic criteria for a major depressive episode within four weeks of childbirth. If the mother's symptoms meet criteria for a psychotic disorder (e.g. hallucinations, delusions) then a diagnosis of a brief psychotic episode with postpartum onset (i.e. postpartum psychosis) could be given.

Page 1332. *Add to footnote 21*:

Also see, D. West, B. Lichtenstein (2006). Andrea Yates and the Criminalization of the Filicidal Maternal Body. *Feminist Criminology*, 1, 173–187.

Page 1332. *Add to footnote 23*:

Much of the confusion stems from the fact that there is no category for "postpartum disorders" in the DSM–IV–TR. Rather the specifier of postpartum onset is given to diagnosed mood or psychotic disorders if onset is within four weeks postpartum. For example, the official label for postpartum psychosis would be brief psychotic episode with postpartum onset.

§ 21.06   Determining Competence to Stand Trial

2.   THE DETERMINATION OF COMPETENCE

Page 1337. *Add to footnote 6*:

For a detailed overview of psychiatric guidelines for determining competence see, D. Mossman and colleagues (2007). AAPL Practice Guideline for the Forensic Psychiatric Evaluation of Competence to Stand Trial. *Journal of the American Academy of Psychiatry and Law*, 35 3–72.

Page 1338. *Add to footnote 11*:

For a detailed review of existing standardized tests of competence and a newly developed instrument see, D. Nussbaum and colleagues (2007) Fitness/Competency to Stand Trial: A Conceptual Overview, Review of Existing Instruments, and Cross–Validation of the Nussbaum Fitness Questionnaire. *Brief Treatment and Crisis Intervention*, 8, 43–72.

III. OTHER FACTORS IN MITIGATION OF DEFENDANT LIABILITY

§ 21.08   "Syndrome" Evidence to Bolster the Prosecutor's Case

1. THE RAPE TRAUMA SYNDROM (RTS)

Page 1343. *Add to footnote 1*:

Also see, K. A. Lonsway and L. S. Fitz-gerald (1994). Rape Myths in Review. *Psychology of Women Quarterly*, 18, 133–164.

§ 21.09   Evidence of Other "Mental" Abnormalities

3. PREMENSTRUAL SYNDROME (PMS)

Page 1352. *Update to footnote 21*:

The DSM–IV is now in its text revised version: DSM–IV–TR. However, there have been no changes to the classification of Premenstrual Dysphoric Disorder since the previous version.

Page 1352. *Add to footnote 23*:

See also, E. W. Freeman (2003). Premenstrual syndrome and premenstrual dysphoric disorder: Definitions and diagnosis. *Psychoneuroendocrinology*, 28, 25–37.

4. EVIDENCE OF OTHER "SYNDROMES"

Page 1356. *Update to footnote 37*:

The DSM–IV is now in its text revised version: DSM–IV–TR. However, there have been no changes to the classification of "Posttraumatic Stress Disorder" since the previous version.

IV. INVOLUNTARY CIVIL COMMITMENT AND THE CONCEPT OF "FUTURE DANGEROUSNESS"

§ 21.13　The Prediction of Future Dangerousness

Page 1363. *Add to footnote 1*:

For a review of the topic of future dangerousness see, P. Woods, G. C. Lasiuk (2008). Risk Prediction: A review of the Literature. *Journal of Forensic Nursing*, 4, 1–11.

V.　MISCELLANEOUS

§ 21.15　Bibliography of Additional References

1.　BOOKS

Update to list of books:

Gary Melton, et al., *Psychological Evaluations for the Courts: A Handbook for Mental Health Professionals and Lawyers*, 3rd ed. 2007.

Vernon Lewis Quinsey, et al., *Violent Offenders: Appraising and Managing Risk*, 2nd ed. 2005.

Christopher Slobogin, Arti Rai, & Ralph Reisner *Law and the Mental Health System*, 5th ed. 2008.

2.　ARTICLES

The recently released WILEY ENCYCLOPEDIA OF FORENSIC SCIENCE (Jamieson, A. & Moenssens, A.A., eds.), 2009, contains over 90 articles as part of its Behavioral Science section. Because the volumes were not yet received at the time this Supplement was prepared, no mention of specific articles contained in its 5 volumes is attempted. The print edition is also expected to become available in 2010 in online format and updated annually.

Chapter 22

EXPERT EVIDENCE ON WITNESS ACCURACY AND THE DETECTION OF DECEPTION

PART I—EYEWITNESSES AND MEMORY

II. THE ISSUE OF TRUSTWORTHINESS OF EYEWITNESS RECOLLECTION

§ 22.02 The Inherent Unreliability of Eyewitnesses—True or False?

Page 1373. *Add to footnote 4*:

Also see, G. L. Wells, & E. A. Olson (2003). Eyewitness Testimony. *Annual Review of Psychology*, 54, 277–293.

§ 22.03 Perception, Memory and Recollection

1. INFLUENCE OF EVENT FACTORS

Page 1375. *Add to paragraph 2*:

The presence of a weapon has also been shown to hinder a witness' ability to identify a perpetrator. See, T.H. Kramer and colleagues (1990).Weapon Focus, Arousal, and Eyewitness Memory. *Law and Human Behavior*, 14, 167–184; G. L. Wells, & E. A. Olson (2003). Eyewitness Testimony. *Annual Review of Psychology*, 54, 277–293.

Page 1375. *Add to footnote 8*:

Also see, K. A. Deffenbacher et al. (2004). A Meta–Analytic Review of the Effects of High Stress on Eyewitness Memory, *Law and Human Behavior*, 28, 687–706.

Page 1376. *Add to footnote 13*:

G. L. Wells & E. A. Olson (2003). Eyewitness Testimony. *Annual Review of Psychology*, 54, 277–293.

3. INFLUENCE OF STORAGE FACTORS

Page 1376. *Add to footnote 15*:

S. Werner & J. Diedrichson (2002). The Time Course of Spatial Memory Distortions. *Memory and Cognition*, 30, 718–730.

Page 1377. *Add to footnote 17:*

K. A. Deffenbacher (1980). Eyewitness Accuracy and Confidence: Can we Infer Anything about Their Relationship? *Law and Human Behavior*, 4, 243–260.

4.   INFLUENCE OF RECALL FACTORS

Page 1377. *Add to footnote 21:*

Also see, G. L. Wells et al. (1998). Eyewitness Identification Procedures: Recommendations for Lineups and Photospreads. *Law and Human Behavior*, 22, 603–647.

Page 1378. *Add to footnote 24:*

B. L. Cutler, et al. (1990). Juror Sensitivity to Eyewitness Identification Evidence *Law and Human Behavior*, 14, 185–191.

§ 22.07   Path of the Future for Eyewitness Evidence

Page 1383. *Add to footnote 2:*

M. S. Zeedyk and F. E. Rait (1998). Psychological Evidence in the Courtroom: Critical Reflections on the General Acceptance Standard. *Journal of Community & Applied Social Psychology*, 8, 23–39.

———

III.   EXPERT EVIDENCE ON THE ACCURACY OF CHILD WITNESSES

§ 22.09   Abilities and Limitations of Child Witnesses

1.   MNEMONIC ACCURACY

Page 1385. *Add to footnote 2:*

For an overview of childhood memory development see, S. E. Gathercole (1998). The Development of Memory. *Journal of Child Psychology and Psychiatry*, 39, 3–27.

2.   SUGGESTIBILITY

Page 1386. *Add to footnote 4:*

S. Ceci and M. Bruck (1993). Suggestibility of the Child Witness: A Historical Review and Synthesis. *Psychological Bulletin*, 113, 403–439.

PART II—DETECTING DECEPTION

———

IV. THE POLYGRAPH TECHNIQUE

§ 22.17 Criticisms of the Polygraph Technique

Page 1402. *Add to footnote 2*:

K. Fiedler, J. Schmid, and T. Stahl (2002). What Is the Current Truth About Polygraph Lie Detection? *Basic and Applied Social Psychology*, 24, 313–324.

———

VI. HYPNOSIS

§ 22.21 Nature and Limitations

Page 1409. *Add to footnote 3*:

Also see, G. F. Wagstaff (2008). Hypnosis and the Law: Examining the Stereotypes. *Criminal Justice and Behavior*, 35, 1277–1294.

———

IX. MISCELLANEOUS

§ 22.33 Books

Update to list of books:

B.L. Bottoms et al., *Children, Social Science, and the Law*, 2nd ed. 2005.

Stanley L. Brodsky, *The Expert Expert Witness: More Guidelines and Maxims for Testifying in Court*, 1999.

J.T. Cacioppo et al., eds., *Handbook of Psychophysiology*, 3rd ed. 2007.

Stephen J. Ceci & Maggie Bruck, *Jeopardy in the Courtroom: A Scientific Analysis of Children's Testimony*, 2nd ed. 1999.

H. Dent & B.L. Flin, *Children as Witnesses*, 2nd ed. 1996.

Lawrence S. Wrightsman & Solomon M. Fulero, *Forensic Psychology*, 3rd ed. 2008.

Lawrence S. Wrightsman, et al., *Psychology and the Legal System* 6th ed. 2006.

§ 22.34 Articles

The recently released WILEY ENCYCLOPEDIA OF FORENSIC SCIENCE (Jamieson, A. & Moenssens, A.A., eds.), 2009, contains over 90 articles as part of its Behavioral Science section. Because the volumes were not yet received at the time this Supplement was prepared, no mention of specific articles contained in its 5 volumes is attempted. The print edition is also expected to become available in 2010 in online format and updated annually.

Chapter 23

BEHAVIORAL EVIDENCE IN PROCEEDINGS INVOLVING CHILDREN AND FAMILIES

II. CHILD CUSTODY

§ 23.02 Conceptual Models and Standards for Determination of Child Custody

Page 1426. *Update to footnote 4*:

Melvin G. Goldzband, *Custody Cases and Expert Witnesses: A Manual for Attorneys* (2nd ed.), 1988.

Page 1426. *Add to footnote 5*:

On the issue, generally, see also, Julie E. Artis, "Judging the Best Interests of the Child: Judges' Accounts of the Tender Years Doctrine," *Law and Society Review*, 38, 796–806.

Page 1427. *Update to footnote 6*:

Joseph Goldstein, et al., *Beyond the Best Interests of the Child* (Revised Ed.), 2004; Joseph Goldstein, et al., *Before the Best Interests of the Child* (Paperback Ed.), 2004.

Page 1427. *Add to footnote 7*:

Also see, Margo A. Kushner "Is 'best interests' a solution to filling potholes in child custody planning?" *Journal of Child Custody*, 3, 71–90.

Page 1428. *Add to footnote 9*:

For additional critiques of the best interests standard, see also, Daniel A. Krauss & Bruce D. Sales "Legal Standards Expertise, and Experts in the Resolution of Contested Child Custody Cases," *Psychology, Public Policy, and Law*, 6, 843–879.

§ 23.03 The Role of Mental Health Experts

Page 1429. *Update to footnote 2*:

Blau, *The Psychologist as the Expert Witness* (2nd ed.), 2001.

Page 1429. *Update to footnote 3*:

Daniel W. Shuman, *Psychiatric and Psychological Evidence* (2nd ed.), 1994.

2. CUSTODY EVALUATIONS

Page 1431. *Update to footnote 5*:

Gary B. Melton, et al., *Psychological Evaluations for the Courts: A Handbook for Mental Health Professionals* (3rd ed.), 2007.

3. USE OF PSYCHIATRIC AND PSYCHOLOGICAL TESTS

Page 1432. *Update to footnote 9*:

Richard A. Gardner, *Family Evaluation in Child Custody: Mediation Arbitration and Litigation* (Updated and Revised Ed.) 1989.

§ 23.05 Parental Alienation Syndrome

Page 1436. *Update to footnote 4*:

Eleanor E. Maccoby & Robert H. Mnookin, *Dividing the Child–Social and Legal Dilemmas of Custody* (2nd Ed.), 1994.

§ 23.06 Use of the Expert in Court

Page 1437. *Update to footnote 1*:

Black's Law Dictionary (8th Ed.), 2004.

―――――

III. DOMESTIC VIOLENCE

§ 23.08 Current Scientific Knowledge on the Nature of Domestic Violence

Page 1439. *Update to footnote 3*:

Martin Seligman, *Helplessness: On Depression, Development, and Death (Reprint)*, 1992.

Page 1440. *Add to footnote 6*:

Also see, E. Peled, P. G. Jaffe, & J. L. Edleson (eds.), *Ending the Cycle of Violence: Community Responses to Children of Battered Women*, 1994.

§ 23.10 The Battered Spouse Syndrome as Defense or Diminished Capacity

1. DEVELOPMENT OF THE SYNDROME

Page 1442. *Update to footnote 4*:

Lenore Walker, *The Battered Woman Syndrome* (3rd Ed. Rev.), 2008.

Page 1442. *Update to footnote 6:*

Lenore Walker, *Terrifying Love: Why Battered Women Kill and How Society Responds* (Reprint) 1990.

2. SELF–DEFENSE AND THE BATTERED SPOUSE

Page 1442. *Update to footnote 9:*

Lafave, W., *Criminal Law* (Hornbook Series Student 4th Ed.), 2003.

————

IV. CHILD ABUSE AND NEGLECT

§ 23.12 Child Abuse and Neglect Proceedings

Page 1449. *Update to footnote 1:*

Cynthia Crosson–Tower, *Understanding Child Abuse and Neglect* (7th Ed.), 2007.

§ 23.13 Exposure to Domestic Violence

Page 1449. *Update to footnote 1:*

M. Straus, et al., *Behind Closed Doors: Violence in the American Family* (2nd Ed.), 2006.

Page 1449. *Update to footnote 4:*

Osofsky (Ed.), *Children in a Violent Society* (Paperback Ed.), 1998.

Page 1450. *Update to footnote 7:*

Yllo & Bogard (Eds.), *Feminist Perspectives on Wife Abuse* (2nd Ed.), 2007.

Page 1450. *Update to footnote 10:*

Osofsky (Ed.), *Children in a Violent Society* (Paperback Ed.), 1998.

————

V. JUVENILE ADJUDICATIONS

§ 23.15 The Nature of Juvenile Court

Page 1452. *Update to footnote 1*:

Cynthia Crosson–Tower, *Understanding Child Abuse and Neglect* (7th Ed.), 2007.

§ 23.16 The Role of Experts in Juvenile Court

Page 1453. *Add to footnote 1*:

Also see, Ivan Kruh & Thomas *Grisso, Evaluation of Juveniles'* Competence to Stand Trial: Best Practices in *Forensic Mental Health Assessment*, 2008.

———

VI. MISCELLANEOUS

§ 23.17 Bibliography of Additional References

1. BOOKS

Update to list of books:

Bette L. Bottoms, et al., *Children, Social Science, and the Law* (2nd Ed.), 2005.

Howard Dubowitz & Dianne DePanfilis, *The Handbook for Child Protection Practice*, Paperback Ed., 2000.

Thomas Grisso & Robert G. Schwartz (Eds.), *Youth on Trial*, Paperback Ed., 2003.

Cindy L. Miller–Perrin & Robin D. Perrin, *Child Maltreatment: An Introduction* (2nd Ed.), 2006.

2. ARTICLES

The recently released Wiley Encyclopedia of Forensic Science (Jamieson, A. & Moenssens, A.A., eds.), 2009, contains over 90 articles as part of its Behavioral Science section. Because the volumes were not yet received at the time this Supplement was prepared, no mention of specific articles contained in its 5 volumes is attempted. The print edition is also expected to become available in 2010 in online format and updated annually.

†